A Call To Prayer

Intercession in Action

by
Germaine Copeland

A Call to Prayer
Intercession in Action
ISBN 0-89274-855-9

Copyright © 1997 by Germaine Copeland
Word Ministries, Inc.

Published by Harrison House, Inc.
P. O. Box 35035
Tulsa, Oklahoma 74153

Printed in the United States of America.
All rights reserved under International Copyright Law. Contents and/or cover may not be reproduced in whole or in part in any form without the express written consent of the Publisher.

Harrison House
Tulsa, Oklahoma

4th Printing
Over 29,000 in Print

A Call to Prayer
Intercession in Action
ISBN 0-89274-855-9
(Revised, Formerly ISBN 0-89274-440-5,
Copyright © 1987.)
Copyright © 1991 by Word Ministries, Inc.
P. O. Box 76532
Atlanta, Georgia 30358

Published by Harrison House, Inc.
P. O. Box 35035
Tulsa, Oklahoma 74153

And this is the confidence that we have in him, that, if we ask any thing according to his will, he heareth us:

And if we know that he hear us, whatsoever we ask, we know that we have the petitions that we desired of him.

1 John 5:14,15 KJV

DEDICATION

This book is dedicated to my Dad, A. H. "Buck" Griffin:

An upright man, a holy man, a man that Jesus made,
To point lost souls to Calvary so they too might be saved.
An honest man who has given his life to the One Who
*   never changes,*
Because just like Him, he is always the same,
Today, yesterday and forever, if you ever thought him
*   strange.*

Now this is the man who directed me to the way, the
*   truth, and the life.*
Oh! What a redemptive plan;
To be born to a man, then born again, escaping a heathen
*   land.*
In high esteem and respect I do hold you, your life has
*   only begun,*
As your Father looks down and says to you, "Keep tell-
*   ing the truth, My son."*

— Beverly Ann Bramlett
Sister of Germaine Copeland, President —
Word Ministries, Inc.

CONTENTS

Contents

ACKNOWLEDGMENTS

If I were to acknowledge everyone who has helped me in my search for knowledge on intercessory prayer, the list of names would be quite lengthy. It is with joy that I remember each one who has been in Word Ministries' prayer groups, and those who have shared many learning experiences with me. I have learned from everyone who has been a part of my life, and to them I offer my thanks and appreciation. The Holy Spirit has been my greatest Teacher, and I can say with thankfulness of heart, ''Our Father has done great and mighty things.''

I would be remiss if I did not first of all give honor to my husband, Everette, who has exercised much patience and loving kindness during the writing of this book. He has been a source of counsel and encouragement throughout our 32 years of marriage. It has been his love and support that have enabled me to obey God's call on my life as a wife, mother, pastor, teacher and writer. Together we have seen our four children grow up in the love of God, and today they are all serving Him. Our son and his precious wife have given us four beautiful grandchildren. Our posterity truly belongs to God.

Many thanks to Dorothy Woodhall who has taken care of the business affairs for Word Ministries,

Incorporated, running references, both typing and printing prayers, and being a sounding board for many ideas. Above all else, her prayers and love have given me the strength and courage needed to get this book written. Whenever I was tempted to become discouraged, it was Dottie who reminded me of the great things God has done.

Without my friend and editor, Donna Walker, this book would never have reached the publisher. Her God-given abilities for writing, organization and editing have helped make this publication available to the Body of Christ. The Father truly knitted us together in the bonds of love, gave us one mind, and brought us into one accord so that no concept was ever tampered with or altered. The family of God is enriched by her obedience to the Father.

I must not neglect to mention my friend, Carole Price, who has been willing to listen, and who furnished a peaceful place at the beach for me to be quiet before God and accomplish the writing of this book. Her critique and encouragement have enabled me to continue in the things to which God has called me.

Last, but not least, I wish to express my love and gratitude to my mother, Donnis Griffin, who is my friend and confidante. She is always there to cry with me, laugh with me, and give me wise counsel. Her diligence, discipline and faithfulness to a life of prayer have been an inspiration and an example of stability in my life. She and my dad, to whom this book is dedicated, are living memorials to God. They taught me that God answers prayer.

INTRODUCTION

Intercessory prayer is prayer offered on behalf of another person (or other persons) as an expression of love. Jesus said, **Greater love hath no man than this, that a man lay down his life for his friends** (John 15:13 KJV). Intercession is a manifestation of that God-kind of love.

In Ephesians 6:12 KJV we discover that, as Christians, **. . . we wrestle not against flesh and blood, but against principalities, against powers, against the rulers of the darkness of this world, against spiritual wickedness in high places.** Then the Apostle Paul, the writer of this epistle, goes on to tell us about the armor which God has provided for us to use in our spiritual warfare. This armor is the same prayer armor that Jesus wore when He came to earth as the Intercessor for all mankind. (Is. 59:16,17.)

In other scripture passages Paul tells us that we should be praying all manner of prayers (or all kinds of prayers) at every opportunity, not only for all the saints but for all men everywhere. (Eph. 6:18; 1 Tim. 2:1.) This book is written not to discourage intercession, but to expose its abuse and neglect and to influence believers to look to the Word of God for sound doctrine, reproof, correction and instruction. (2 Tim. 3:15.)

11

I was led to establish a ministry which was born out of intercessory prayer. The different kinds of prayers mentioned in the Bible have been experienced in this ministry as the Holy Spirit has taught those of us involved in it to pray "prayers that avail much." (James 5:16.)

Satan will do all in his power to stop the flow of the Spirit which is released through prayer. Remember, there is no distance in the spirit world. That prayer you offer up in your present location can strike like lightning in another part of the world, bringing about the plan and purpose of God.

When you begin to pray, you become a part of the present-day ministry of Jesus Christ, . . . **seeing he ever liveth to make intercession . . . .** (Heb. 7:25 KJV). Through prayer, you and I become His voice in the earth. With the help of the Holy Spirit, we become co-laborers with our heavenly Father.

Intercession begins with an act of an individual's will in obedience to the Father God and is a spiritual exercise. The two most valuable tools in intercession are: 1) *the Word of God,* and 2) *prayer in the spirit:*

> **And this is the confidence that we have in him** (God), **that, if we ask any thing according to his will, he heareth us:**
>
> **And if we know that he hear us, whatsoever we ask, we know that we have the petitions that we desired of him.**
>
> **1 John 5:14,15 KJV**

God's will is His Word. The Word of God is spirit and brings life. Praying in other tongues is praying in the language of the spirit rather than in the language of the mind. It moves the person out of the natural (physical) realm into the supernatural (spiritual) realm. This enables him to pray beyond his own limited human knowledge and ability by releasing the Holy Spirit within him. The Spirit of the Lord is then free to bear the intercessor up, to express the mind and will of God through him, and to help him produce supernatural results.

Since the Holy Spirit knows the will and plan of God, He can assist you when you pray in tongues by helping you to hold and express the thoughts, feelings, and purposes of God's own heart. By cooperating with the Holy Spirit, you enable Him to aid you in praying the fulfillment of God's purpose.

Say with the Apostle Paul, . . . **I will pray with the spirit, and I will pray with the understanding** (the mind) **also . . . .** (1 Cor. 14:15 KJV). That is God's overall scriptural plan for effective prayer.

However, it is not my intention in these pages to try to establish any set *methods* or *formulas* for that effective prayer. Rather, my desire is simply to share with you some insights which the Holy Spirit has taught me over the past several years about this subject. The instruction herein applies both to individual prayers of positive confession and intercession, as well as to group prayers of this type. Even though I am able to share some truths with you through the medium of the printed page, the only way you will ever really learn about prayer is to get actively involved in it yourself. It is then that your personal Teacher and Guide, the Holy Spirit, can begin to give you wisdom and spiritual understanding in this vital area.

When I first made a decision to act on God's Word concerning prayer, it was an overwhelming project. At that time my family was experiencing a crisis situation in our home which could only be set right by divine intervention brought about through someone committed to prayer. That someone had to be me — there was no one else to do it. From that experience I learned that not only does God tell us in His Word *how* to pray, He also tells us *who* is called to pray, and *the way* to enter into this important phase of ministry.

This is the practical, spiritual knowledge which I would like to share with you in this book.

1
FORMS OF INTERCESSION

Intercession is manifested in various forms. It is imperative that our intercession places us in agreement with God. We establish agreement with the Lord by articulating His Word. Through the words of the Apostle Paul, our Father has given instruction in 1 Timothy 2:1,2 KJV for the kind of prayer practice that will assure us a quiet and peaceable life, which is His will for us:

> I exhort therefore, that, first of all, supplications, prayers, intercessions, and giving of thanks, be made for all men;
>
> For kings, and for all that are in authority; that we may lead a quiet and peaceable life in all godliness and honesty.

As Christians we are to involve ourselves in the affairs of God and man through intercession. In the Name of Jesus, we come boldly before the throne of grace, approaching God in faith and confidence, addressing Him in familiar but respectful conversational language, asking that His will be done on earth as it is in heaven. In order to converse with God, we must learn to speak as God speaks, because we are told that if we ask anything according to His will, he hears us.

15

(1 John 5:14,15.) To know God's will, we must study and know His written Word. His will is revealed to us in His Word — so His will *is* His Word.

Our confidence toward God is strong when we know what *He* says about the situations for which we are praying. He has given us the mind of Christ. He has also provided us with His written Word so that His mind can be developed within us as we read, study and meditate upon the Scriptures.

For instance, let's look at what the Bible has to say about the will of God for mankind. First Timothy 2:4 tells us that God wishes for all men to be saved, and to come into the full knowledge of the truth. Therefore, we can pray for the salvation of others, in full confidence that by so doing we are praying in agreement with the Word and will of God. Then we can be assured: 1) that the Lord of the harvest hears our prayer, (1 John 5:14); 2) that He will send forth laborers into His harvest fields who will share the Good News of the Gospel with the lost, (Matt. 9:38); 3) that those who hear and believe will be delivered from the authority of darkness and translated into the kingdom of God's dear Son. (Col. 1:13).

After we pray for all men, we can then pray the following prayer for those in authority over us:

> Father, I intercede on behalf of those in positions of authority, seeking Your intervention in the affairs of their lives.
>
> Father, I pray that the uncompromisingly righteous be in authority in our country so that the people can rejoice. I pray that their offices be established and be made secure by righteousness. I pray that right and just

lips be a delight to those in authority, and that they love those who speak what is right.

In the Name of Jesus, amen.

Praying in the Spirit

Many people never experience the depth of this second phase of intercession because of wrong teaching, fear, or lack of knowledge. In Romans 8:26,27 KJV we read:

> **Likewise, the Spirit also helpeth our infirmities: for we know not what we should pray for as we ought: but the Spirit itself maketh intercession for us with groanings which cannot be uttered.**
>
> **And he that searcheth the hearts knoweth what is the mind of the Spirit, because he maketh intercession for the saints according to the will of God.**

When you do not know how to pray about a certain situation, that is the appropriate time to use your prayer language — to pray in a tongue that is unknown to your natural mind. When you have exhausted your conscious knowledge of the situation, there is still Someone Who knows every aspect of the case. He also knows the mind of the Father in a way that is far above and beyond your natural understanding. Your praying in the spirit — in an unknown tongue — enables the Holy Spirit to assist you in achieving His desired results.

Let me share with you an experience that I believe will help to illustrate this "deeper level" of intercession.

One day as I was praying for a certain minister, I began by saying, "Father, I don't know how to pray for this man according to the prophecies that have been spoken concerning him — and I don't know anything else to pray.'' (Have you ever been in that situation?) Then, after a short time of praying in the spirit, I was aware that the Spirit of God was helping me to pray. There were heart-rending sobs which I was uttering in a language which I had never expressed before in prayer.

After an interval of time, I began to pray in my native English. As I listened, I found myself saying (again by the Spirit of God), ''Father, I thank You that this man is not ready to be offered up, that his time of departure is not at hand, that it is only after the fulfill-ment of all prophecies that he will say, 'I have fought a good fight, I have finished my course, I have kept the faith.' Then, Father, he will receive the crown of righteousness which You have laid up for him on that day.''

Great rejoicing came forth from within me as I laughed, clapped my hands, and danced about. Later, I found out that Satan had tried to convince this particular minister that he was finished, that no one wanted to hear what he had to say, that there was no longer a place for him in the Body of Christ. A spirit of death had tried to overtake him.

Only the Spirit of God could have known these things. It was the Holy Spirit Who was searching out the heart of this individual and Who also knew the plan of God for him. While the enemy was working against him with thoughts contrary to the will of God, the Spirit of the Lord was working on His behalf through someone who would give herself to prayer. Through this cooperative intercession between a willing believer and the Holy Spirit, the strategy and plan of the enemy were exposed and thwarted.

Praying in Travail

Another form of intercession is travail. Even though some people do not believe that travail is necessary, in his letter to the Galatian saints Paul opens with these words: **My little children, of whom I travail in birth again until Christ be formed in you** (Gal. 4:19 KJV). Here Paul intimates that he had previously travailed for their spiritual birth, and is now travailing once again for their spiritual development and maturity.

Let's explore this passage of scripture. The Greek word translated *travail* in this verse is *odino*, a verb meaning "to experience the pains of birth." In this context, travail is a spiritual activity. Its purpose is to "bring forth" or to "give birth." As in natural childbirth, we cannot will spiritual travail to take place, nor can we "work it up," as many have tried to do; travail is not a product of the mind, will or emotions.

The prophet Isaiah foretold of the coming Messiah: **He (God) shall see the travail of his (Jesus') soul, and shall be satisfied . . . .** (Is. 53:11 KJV). Jesus was the intercessor Whom God required to suffer the birth pains of redemption for all mankind. God had searched everywhere for a human intercessor and could not find one, so He assumed the responsibility Himself in the form of His Son.

The legal side of redemption was provided for in the death and resurrection of God's Anointed. Today you and I are living on the vital side of redemption. Travail has not passed away, for men will not be saved except an intercessor delivers them out of the authority of darkness and into the kingdom of God's dear Son. Right now, Jesus is seated at the right hand of God the Father in heaven, interceding for man. This intercession is released into the earth through His Body, just as spiritual endowments are released through the believers as the Spirit wills. As servants of Christ, our first priority in prayer is the salvation of mankind, followed by ". . . travail in birth again until Christ be formed in (them) . . . ." bringing deliverance and full maturity. Travail is not a "flaky" manifestation of the flesh, but true travail originates with the Holy Spirit and emanates from the spirit of the intercessor.

Travail is often debated among the churches. My viewpoint is this: let those who travail, travail, and let those who don't, don't. Let's not allow the Church of Jesus Christ to split over this issue.

Travail usually comes forth with groanings and moanings too deep to be uttered in articulate speech. (Rom. 8.) Travail is of the spirit, from the Holy Spirit, and not of the flesh (human nature). However, the flesh (the human mind, will and emotions) can be affected according to an individual's interpretation of the travail process or to his level of spiritual understanding and maturity.

Privately (or in group prayer in which each intercessor has knowledge and understanding of travail), an individual is free to respond physically and emotionally to the workings of the Holy Spirit by yielding to Him his entire being — spirit, soul and body. However, in public we must exercise extreme self-control in this area. We must learn to govern, or hold in check, our human emotions and physical responses. The mistake that has been made in the past is that those who have placed their confidence in physical or emotional manifestations have attempted to *initiate* a work of the spirit by crying, screaming, shaking or moaning. Most of these people will say that they cannot stop this physical or emotional activity; they have thus mistaken their own lack of self-restraint for a sign that they are being irresistibly "moved" by a spiritual force beyond their control.

In 1 Corinthians 14:32 the Apostle Paul reminds us that the spirit of a prophet is subject to the prophet. I believe that the spirit of the intercessor is subject to the intercessor. The Holy Spirit does not "overpower" anyone against his will, nor does He work in a manner to call undue attention to any person or group of people. His job is to glorify Jesus Christ. God's Holy Spirit is not repulsive; He does not drive other people away from Jesus through strange or bizarre activity. Instead, He draws people to Jesus by His actions.

Travail is a cry before the Father and should be done in the prayer closet or with those who have understanding in the area of intercession. Travail emanates from the spirit of man at the impulse of the Holy Spirit; it cannot be "worked up"! In general public worship, you should exercise the self-control which has been given to you by God the Father. (2 Tim. 1:7.)

I have experienced and observed travail in desperate circumstances. One night as I was praying with a friend, she began to travail with a fervor which could not be expressed except in cries and moans. As she travailed, I prayed in the spirit. Through a word

21

of knowledge, the Holy Spirit revealed to us the identity of the couple for whom she was interceding, and the fact that they were in grave danger; it was a life or death situation. After a short period of time, my prayer partner was released from the travail, and the peace of God which passes understanding consumed each of us — spirit, soul and body. This peace ushered us into the rest of God. Deliverance had been brought forth and completed. (Heb. 4:11.)

Later, we learned that on that very day the husband for whom we had been praying had acquired a pistol for the purpose of killing his wife and himself. Satan's plan was thwarted by our intercession, and deliverance was birthed for two people who did not know how to go to God for themselves. God was looking for someone to intercede in behalf of another. He found two people who were willing to yield themselves to the Holy Spirit.

If you are searching for your ministry, begin here — by giving yourself to others through intercessory prayer. Let's not allow the art of intercession to be lost, or stolen from us, through ignorance and neglect. In His Word, God tells us that He will not allow our foot to be caught in a trap or hidden snare. (Prov. 3:26.) His light will dispel the darkness if we are willing to learn from one another. Many hurts and costly mistakes can be avoided if we heed the counsel and advice of those who have walked this way before.

Let's be intercessors. Let's learn to "pray one for another," as our Lord has instructed. (James 5:16.)

2
PURPOSE OF INTERCESSION

The purpose of intercession is to establish the will of the Father in the earth. God's purpose far outreaches the comprehension of the average church-goer. However, within the broad scope of His plan we can approach the Father on behalf of others, praying as He has instructed us, in order that we may lead a quiet and peaceable life and influence the lives of others. Through the medium of prayer we are instrumental in establishing the intercession of Jesus in the earth.

Spirit-Led Intercession Brings Deliverance

One day as I sat down in my den to pray, I felt overwhelmed by the many and various needs of numerous individuals. There were too many names to even mention. As I sat there contemplating how and where to start, I said aloud: "Father, I do not know where to begin today. There are so many needs out there. You know where intercession is most needed at this moment. I present my body to You as a living sacrifice, holy and acceptable unto You, which is my reasonable service and spiritual worship, to pray for whomever You will. Jesus is searching the hearts and, Holy Spirit,

23

according to Romans 8, You know the plan of God for today.''

All of the Godhead is searching our hearts and the hearts of others. If you and I are willing, the Holy Spirit can bring us alongside another who needs spiritual assistance. The Spirit knows the very spot of the heaviest enemy attack and whose heart is crying out for freedom. (Rom. 8:26-27.)

I began to pray in the spirit and after praying for a few minutes, I realized that I was entering into that arena of prayer where the Holy Spirit ''takes hold together with us'' against our infirmities — our inability to produce results. (Rom. 8:26.) I did not even know for whom I was praying, much less the desired results.

In order for you to really appreciate this experience, I need to tell you that for a period of time after our son David was delivered from a life of drugs and all that goes with it, he returned to his old habits. When I realized that he was on drugs again, I said: ''Lord, for seven years I believed for that boy's release and saw him set free after reading the book of Malachi from *The Living Bible* while sitting in his own living room all alone — just he and the Holy Ghost. He has given his testimony and witnessed for You, and now he is bringing a reproach to the Body of Christ. I am through. You will have to raise up another intercessor this time.''

(It does not pay to tell God what you will and won't do. Aren't you glad that God looks on the heart? Through this experience I learned that He has a keen sense of humor.)

As I continued to pray in the spirit, I found myself standing before a building. It was obviously a business, and I recognized where I was because I had been there before. When I walked around the building I saw him, David. There he stood, engrossed in his work. He was totally unaware of three demonic spirits around his head. One had his fingers in David's ears, another had his hands over David's eyes and the third had his arm around David's head as though he were binding something to his mind.

In my boldness, these three presented no problem to me. I was in the spirit and knew that I had been given authority over all the power of the satanic kingdom. I began to speak to those spirits, and when they heard my voice they became very agitated. As I gave them the command to go in the name of Jesus, they left one by one. It was then that I began to pray in English as the Holy Spirit gave me utterance, ministering deliverance, peace and restoration to David's inner man.

When I turned to leave, I saw one of those demons peeking around the corner of the building. I stamped my foot and repeated the command for it to go in the name of Jesus and not return, and it left. It was then that I realized that physically I was still in my home.

A few days later when I talked with David, I asked him if God had been talking to him recently. He shared with me how he had not wanted the other guys to feel that he was self-righteous and had yielded once again to smoking pot. He believed that he could "walk in the middle of the road," remaining a Christian yet taking a smoke when he wanted — after all, he could handle it now.

This kind of thinking is a snare of the enemy which many Christians have fallen into because of a lack of knowledge. David admitted, however, that lately he had become concerned because he realized that he was no longer hearing the voice of God. He continued:

"I woke up the other morning and saw that I was no longer in the middle of the road and was not only on the side, but off the shoulder and into the ditch. I had been confused about the voices which I was hearing and was no longer sure about what was true. This morning I heard God's voice and knew that it was the Lord speaking to me. I heard and understood truth."

Praise the name of Jesus, I had seen the purpose of intercession in action when I cooperated with the Holy Spirit in prayer. Deliverance and restoration were accomplished — the prodigal son had come home. Yes, the Holy Spirit knew where the intercession was most needed that day. The result was the establishment of God's will in "the earth" (the life of our son).

Pleading the Cause of Others

Pleading the cause of others, as in a court case, is another purpose of intercession. (1 Tim. 2:1) Here again, Jesus is our example. Isaiah said of Him, **. . . he bare the sin of many, and made intercession for the transgressors** (Is. 53:12).

When praying for others, it is important to unite with the Spirit. There is power in words, and if we do not pray according to the will of God, we will pray amiss, perhaps delaying or thwarting the fulfillment of God's plan and purpose in the individual's life.

It is imperative that we have the intercession of Jesus revealed to us for those with whom we are emotionally involved, especially our loved ones. This is an area in which our own will and feelings can so easily come into play. When we react emotionally to a situation, allowing pride or emotions to control us, the picture becomes distorted and we may lose sense of the proper manner in which to pray; sometimes we may even find ourselves seeking revenge in certain situations.

Intercession as Defense or Vindication

Another purpose of intercession is to defend or vindicate someone or his actions. We cannot do this while holding anything against the person for whom we are praying. In order to pray for others, we must forgive. Unforgiveness is the number one hindrance to answered prayer.

There was a period of time when I was having difficulty praying for one of our daughters. She had been saved at an early age; later, in her teenage years she was filled with the Holy Spirit. Since the time of her salvation, she had faithfully read her Bible. After she graduated from college, she was different, and I did not like what I was seeing.

While she was still in high school, God performed a miracle in our relationship. We had experienced a communication breakdown. The Spirit of God taught me how to pray for her. I wrote that prayer down and prayed it until the breakthrough came.[1]

---

[1]See "Improving Communication," *Prayers That Avail Much — Volume I* by Word Ministries, Inc. (Tulsa: Harrison House, 1989, p. 126.)

Not only were her attitudes changed, but God taught me more about working out my own salvation with fear and trembling and, as a result, godly changes took place within me.

This was the daughter who had prayed for her mom and dad when we were having a communication problem which looked hopeless: "Jesus is Mom and Dad's peace, and He has made both one, and has broken down the middle wall of partition between them. He has abolished in His flesh the enmity, to make in Himself of the two, one new man, so making peace. He has reconciled both unto God in one body by the cross, having slain the enmity thereby." (Eph. 2:14-16.)

She shared this prayer with me, and we prayed in agreement knowing that Jesus said, **"...if two of you on earth agree about anything you ask for, it will be done for you by my Father in heaven"** (Matt. 18:19 NIV).

It appeared now that in her pursuit of money and pleasure, our daughter had forsaken all that we had taught her, and that God had very little space in her life. I began praying for her, apparently to no avail.

One day my husband said to me: "You have grown very hard toward our daughter, and you are holding things against her. You need to forgive her and continue walking in love."

At first I refused to believe this was true, but God by His Spirit revealed to me that in order for my prayers on her behalf to have any effect, I had to acknowledge my unforgiveness and repent. He reminded me of John 20:23 (NIV): **"...If you forgive anyone his sins, they are forgiven; if you do not forgive them, they are not**

forgiven.'' I had never known how to apply this scripture and was concerned about praying presumptuously or foolishly. It was my heart's desire to pray accurately and according to the intercession of Jesus.

First of all, I asked forgiveness for my attitude toward my daughter, and God was faithful and just to forgive me and cleanse me from all unrighteousness. Then the Holy Spirit led me to release her from her sins. I certainly did not want my child suffering the judgment pronounced on sin. I wanted her delivered. Words began to come forth in English: ''Father, I forgive her and according to Your Word her sins are forgiven. I no longer hold anything against her, and, according to Your Word, neither do You.''

Now, I do not spend very much time talking to the devil, but I do so when it is necessary for him to understand that I am aware of his position in relation to me and the situation for which I am praying. So I told him firmly:

''Satan, you cannot have our daughter nor destroy her. You will not bring affliction upon her. I suppress the judgment that is attached to sin, and declare that she is forgiven. I am now standing in the gap until she comes to her senses and personal repentance. She is part of our household and a partaker of the blood covenant.''

Then I loosed her from the deception and lies of the enemy and released to her ''godly sorrow which worketh repentance to salvation'' that she ''might receive life and that more abundantly.'' (2 Cor. 7:10; John 10:10 KJV.) Then it was time to rejoice and give glory to God for His intervention in her life. She did awake to righteousness and return to the Shepherd of her soul. Glory to God for the great things which He has done.

Intercession in Accordance With God's Will

Our prayers must be in accordance with God's purpose and plan. There was a time when Judah had committed the sin of idolatry. God told Jeremiah that he was not to pray for Judah, neither was he to lift up a cry for them nor make intercession for them. (Jer. 7:16.) Later, Jeremiah did intercede on their behalf, but his prayer was never answered.

There were times when God looked for a man to pray in order to withhold judgment, but it seems that it was not the will of the Father to withhold His judgment from Judah at this time.

In 1 John 5:16,17 KJV, John writes:

> **If any man see his brother sin a sin which is not unto death, he shall ask, and he shall give him life for them that sin not unto death. There is a sin unto death: I do not say that he shall pray for it.**

> **All unrighteousness is sin: and there is a sin not unto death.**

We must know the voice of the Holy Spirit and allow Him to lead us in our praying. We can't just get upset with people and decide that we will withhold intercession from them because we want to see them punished.

> **Recompense to no man evil for evil. . . .**

> **. . . Vengeance is mine; I will repay, saith the Lord.**

> **Romans 12:17,19 KJV**

30

The joyous intercessor is always ready to release the mercy cry, ''Father, forgive them; they know not what they do.'' (Luke 23:34.)

Commending Others to God

In intercession you may commend others to God as in Hebrews 7:25 and Romans 8:26-28. We commend to the Lord our loved ones, as well as others, for salvation, healing, reconciliation and restoration. In intercessory prayer we furnish any kind of assistance or help necessary to establish the eternal plan of God in the earth, being profitable to His Kingdom, positively affecting individuals, communities and nations.

Intercession and God's Eternal Plan

God's overall plan includes the restoration of all things, the manifestation of the sons of God and the fulfillment of His promises to Israel. (Rom. 8-11.)

''The age of grace,'' which is also known as ''the age of the Gentiles,'' is approaching its completion. Soon there will be the catching away of the saints, which is called ''the rapture,'' when we shall see Him as He is. A period of seven years of tribulation will follow, to be consummated at the second advent of Jesus Christ when He returns to earth with His saints. At that time He will establish the Kingdom of heaven in this earthly realm and ''the government shall be upon His shoulder.'' (Is. 9:6.) Israel as a nation will recognize the Messiah, Jerusalem will be His capital, and God's promises to Israel will be fulfilled. (Is. 2:3.) The saints will reign with Him, and Israel will become priests of the Lord to all other nations.

And when all things shall be subdued unto him, then shall the Son also himself be subject unto him that put all things under him, that God may be all in all.

1 Corinthians 15:28 KJV

God's purposes are eternal. We are preparing the way of the Lord as He sets the stage for the millennial reign of Christ.

O the depth of the riches both of the wisdom and knowledge of God! how unsearchable are his judgments, and his ways past finding out!

For who hath known the mind of the Lord? or who hath been his counsellor?

Or who hath first given to him, and it shall be recompensed unto him again?

For of him, and through him, and to him, are all things: to whom be glory for ever. Amen.

Romans 11:33-36 KJV

It is imperative that we continue in faith, cooperating with God's plan, praying always without fainting or turning coward. God's eternal plan will be consummated.

We must remember that it is not people we are to act against; it is the devil and his demons. In J.B. Philips translation of Ephesians 6:11,12 Paul writes:

Put on God's complete armour so that you can successfully resist all the devil's craftiness.

32

> **For** *our fight is not against any physical enemy:*
> *it is against organizations and powers that are*
> *spiritual. We are up against the unseen power that con-*
> *trols this dark world, and spiritual agents from the very*
> *headquarters of evil.*

Our enemies, against whom we wrestle in the spiritual realm, are not flesh and blood. Do not approach God with accusations against your brothers and sisters — they are not your enemies. To pray against any other human being, even our worst enemy, is to misuse the prayer of intercession.

As we have seen, under the Old Covenant, King David considered the enemies of God to be his own personal enemies, and he physically annihilated as many of them as possible. The Old Testament way of dealing with those who opposed God was to execute God's vengeance and wrath upon them. The New Testament saint administers his God-given authority in the spiritual realm, not the physical, aware of the enemy's devices.

Let the high praises of God be in your mouth, and a two-edged sword in your hand to execute vengeance only upon the satanic kingdom. (Ps. 149:6,7). Use intercessory prayer as a spiritual weapon on behalf of those held in bondage by the powers of darkness.

3
GODLY WISDOM FOR INTERCESSION

Art or Idol

Some churches today are in danger of making an "idol" out of intercession and thereby losing the "art" of intercessory prayer. Some have given intercessors a status above all the five-fold ministry gifts: apostles, prophets, evangelists, pastors and teachers. Many of God's people are looking to the intercessor for leadership and guidance, expecting him or her individually (or as a group) to replace the ministry, the Word of God, or even the Holy Spirit.

One church I visited had provided badges to identify their intercessors. It appeared to me they were esteemed a notch above everyone else — including the pastor! An importance was being placed on persons, rather than on the Person of Jesus Christ to Whom it rightfully belongs. I had the distinct impression that the members of that church had forgotten the words of Paul who said we are called . . . **with an holy calling, not according to our works, but according to his own purpose and grace, which was given us in Christ Jesus before the world began** (2 Tim. 1:9 KJV).

Some pastors today are shying away from everyone who claims to be an intercessor. Many unfortunate, sad and regrettable encounters have taken place between pastors and the intercessors in their churches.

During the early days of the Pentecostal movement in our country, personal character weaknesses and abuse of the gifts of the Holy Spirit on the part of some Pentecostals caused many people to reject the experience of the Baptism in the Holy Spirit.

For example, the denomination in which I grew up was deceived into making an idol of speaking in tongues. In my generation, although we talked about the Holy Spirit and speaking in tongues, the average church-goer had no concept of the proper usage and purpose of tongues. The Holy Spirit was regarded as some kind of mystical "force" which mysteriously came upon people, overpowering them with His presence and causing them to do all kinds of weird and unreasonable things. Messages in tongues were given without any interpretation, often at inopportune times, interrupting the service. Sometimes burning oil or kerosene lamps were taken to individuals in the congregation. An unseen force seemingly caused them to pass their hands through the open flames. The act itself was done to prove that the power of God was present and would prevent damage to the body. God in His mercy protected them through their faith. A few actually believed that this was the power of God moving, but many were repelled by these bizarre actions. In that society, when a person spoke in tongues, he was thought to have achieved the ultimate in spiritual maturity.

Likewise, today, there are those who are being deceived concerning intercession. An "office of intercessor" has been established in which persons of weak and unstable character and temperament are provided ample opportunity to abuse a God-given privilege. The result is not unity, harmony and peace in the church; it is chaos, disorder and unrest.

In some instances, so-called intercessors have actually alienated the sheep from the shepherd. There are pastors who have lost control of the prayer groups in their churches because they made the mistake of thinking they could safely "leave the praying to others." The culmination of such disruptive activity is often that the pastor demands that the intercessors leave the church. When this happens, a domino effect of hurt and rejection is set off, affecting many church members, as well as the pastor, as he watches his intercessors not only leave but also take many others with them. This ought not to happen. A house divided against itself cannot stand. (Matt. 12:25.)

Is there an answer? I believe there is. Prayer is a vital pillar in any church or of any spiritual endeavor. Without prayer, a church becomes a social organization, failing to meet the spiritual needs of the congregation. Even though the Word of God may be taught, without prayer it becomes a legalistic form, void of power. *Prayer is essential.* It is also of utmost importance that intercessors be taught, guided and instructed in the art of intercession — in love and with wisdom. One of Satan's plans for the destruction of the Church is to remove from the Body of Christ effective prayer, as well as "divers tongues" and all other spiritual weapons.

The first prayer group of which I was leader became misled by familiar spirits. Our only salvation was our honest hearts and our fervent prayer that God would remove all unfavorable information from our minds so that we would never reveal what had been shown to us. It was our sincere desire to see those for whom we were interceding free from demonic oppression. We were relentless in our pursuit of learning how to pray "prayers that avail much." The Holy Spirit, our Teacher, began to show us in the seventeenth chapter of the Gospel of John how Jesus interceded for us. Also, He revealed to us that Paul prayed numerous prayers of intercession which we could use as a model.

When we do not know how to pray, we have a Helper, the Holy Spirit. (Rom. 8:26.) Be determined to follow the Spirit of God. Listen to the inner witness and study the Word of God. Trust the Spirit to guide you into all truth by taking the "things" (the ways) of Jesus and revealing them to you, showing you things to come. (John 16:13,14.)

The anointing of God is on His Word. Praying the Word of God and praying in tongues will break every yoke of bondage. We must be willing to rebuke the evil spirits which would try to invade and control our prayer sessions. Valuable time can be wasted on information that the Holy Spirit would never reveal about a person. Since we are not ignorant of the devises of the enemy, let us look at some of the pitfalls designed to stop the "art" of intercession.

Pitfalls of Intercession
Lack of Knowledge

I bear them witness that they have a [certain] zeal and enthusiasm for God, but it is not enlightened

and according to [correct and vital] knowledge.

Romans 10:2

The zeal of many Christians far exceeds their ability to rightly divide the Word of God. Zeal and enthusiasm are necessary in maintaining an effective prayer life, but without revelation knowledge of the Word of God, the intercessor becomes subject to the designs of the devil. God's Word is truth, and when an individual is seeking truth, God will get that truth to him. Jesus said that His sheep know the voice of the Good Shepherd. We cannot know His voice apart from His Word.

In my early days of searching for the truth about how to pray prayers that would avail much, I attended several different prayer groups. I learned more about what *not* to do than what to do.

At one church prayer meeting, a young lady, who was a new Christian, wanted the group to pray that a certain mountain of difficulty in her life would be removed and cast into the sea. She went on to reveal that the "mountain" she was referring to was her husband. So dutifully everyone in the group began to pray earnestly that this young woman's husband would be "removed" and "cast into the sea"!

From the account she gave, it was obvious that the problem was that the poor man was simply tired of sitting home alone night after night while his wife was out attending prayer meetings, church services, Bible studies, and seminars. Finally, he had asked her to stay home with him, and for that she had informed him that he was the devil. Understandably, a heated discussion then ensued in the home.

Much zeal in praying about the "removal" of her "problem" was displayed in the prayer session, but a lack of revelation was evident. The leader of the group was responsible for instructing that young lady and the intercessors in revelation knowledge and the proper manner in which to pray in this instance. The pastor of the church was not present, and I don't know if he knew how this prayer meeting was being conducted.

Intercession is a serious business. It can either be a vital asset to a church, or a detriment to the spiritual condition and reputation of that ministry. Christians need to adhere to Paul's admonition in 1 Thessalonians 5:12: **. . . get to know those who labor among you — recognize them for what they are . . . .** Those who desire to be in a prayer group should be students of the Word of God and willing to submit to the leader who relies on the written Word for guidance and confirmation. This leader should be capable of teaching revelation knowledge of the scriptures concerning how to pray effectively and how to properly submit to the pastor or to church doctrines.

Misuse of Scriptures

In most prayer groups, the prayer of agreement, as presented by Jesus in Matthew 18:19 KJV, is one of the most misunderstood and abused concepts in the Bible:

> **Again I say unto you, That if two of you shall agree on earth as touching any thing that they shall ask, it shall be done for them of my Father which is in heaven.**

The Lord taught me much about this scripture after a vivid experience in my marriage. The intercessors in

40

the prayer group which I had organized agreed with me that my husband, Everette, would agree to go with me to an upcoming seminar I wanted us to attend together.

At this time Everette did not seem to be interested in the work God had called me to do. (I was seeking more and more of Jesus, and would go with friends or alone to hear various Bible teachers.) Although he refused to go with me, Everette did not hinder me from going. After a while my desire to have my husband attend these meetings with me became a consuming fire within me. Many times when alone, I cried all the way to a service because I wanted my life's partner by my side. I tried everything! I would hear testimonies of how God was bringing couples into total harmony and agreement. I even saw it happening in the marriages of some of the ladies who were attending the Bible study which I was teaching.

Everette ignored all my pleas and the devices to which I resorted in my efforts to get him to go with me. At last, I made my request to the group for prayer for my situation. I was sure that my "time" had arrived because the intercessors entered into that prayer of agreement with me. There was no doubt in my mind that Everette would go. I believed the Bible! Hadn't Jesus said that "anything" that we ask in agreement would be done for us of the Father?

The first night of the meeting came and went. But Everette did not. He stayed at home, and I attended with friends. The second night came and went. Everette did not budge. I attended with friends. Finally, it was the third and closing night of the meeting — God's last chance to answer our "binding" prayer of agreement. Two seats were reserved in the front row of the auditorium — one for me, and one for my husband. As the time for the service approached that evening, I turned down all offers of a ride to the meeting because I just *knew* that my night of triumph had arrived.

It was past time to leave for the meeting and I was still waiting, sure that Everette was going. Finally, he turned to me and said, "If you are going to the service tonight, you'd better leave. You're already late."

I struggled to open my mouth in protest that he just *had* to go with me, but before I could form the words, he closed the subject: "You need to know that you and your friends cannot 'confess' me into going. My mind is made up; I am staying home to watch the World Series on television."

At the meeting I was met by an usher who walked me down that long aisle to the reserved seats while everyone's eyes followed me step by step. I knew that God could not fail, so I was convinced that we must have missed God somewhere. Still, I couldn't understand where we had gone wrong. The intercessors and I had done everything we knew how to do, and on top of that, we believed. Besides, hadn't I put "corresponding action" to my faith by refusing all rides to the meeting? I had acted in accordance to my faith, and that was *supposed* to be the measure of what I received.

There was no lack of zeal on *my* part — or that of the intercessors. But there was also no Everette at the meeting.

Yes, my friends and I had zeal. However, our zeal for God was not enlightened according to correct and vital knowledge. Without that knowledge, our zeal was worthless. Because of a lack of revelation knowledge we had misused the prayer of agreement. We had tried to take scripture out of context, "confess" our own selfish desire, and then expect God to act in response to our misguided "faith." He won't do it. God will not move contrary to His Word in order to answer an improper prayer.

When you are searching for truth, the spirit of error cannot prevail for long. God is patient with His people and gives the Holy Spirit to us to instruct us. In this instance, the Spirit began to do His work of enlightenment in me. One word kept coming to my mind, a word I was increasingly sure was God's answer to my question of where we had gone wrong. The Spirit showed me that in that case what the intercessors and I had engaged in was not spiritual intercession but *manipulation.* Our "spiritual prayer of agreement" had actually been nothing more than an act of the flesh — one which Paul refers to in Galatians 5:20 KJV as "witchcraft"! We had tried to control another person's actions by use of the intellect through prayer and positive confession. I realized that it was not my friends' agreement that I had needed in that situation — it was Everette's!

That night I released my husband's "freedom of choice" to God. I too was set free. I realized that my husband was not against me, but for me. I returned to him what he had given me — the freedom to hear from God and to obey the voice of the Good Shepherd *as an individual.* The very next year another seminar was scheduled, and to my surprise Everette not only attended voluntarily, he also served as an usher by his own volition. I went with him to all the evening services.

All prayer must be based on scripture. If you are praying for your mate, pray according to God's Word, not according to your plans which are usually selfish and for your own benefit. You should learn how to love unconditionally and accept your spouse just as God accepted you. My desire and prayer for Everette became: "Our Father which art in heaven, hallowed be Thy Name. Thy kingdom come. Thy will be done in Everette's life, as it is in heaven." The Holy Spirit gave me many other scriptures of support for this prayer. (See the prayers "Husbands" in *Prayers That Avail Much — Volume I*,[1] and "The New Creation Marriage," in *Prayers That Avail Much — Volume II*.[2]) God forgave me for attempting to usurp my husband's authority and free will.

The only person who never makes a mistake is the one who never does anything. Thank God that **every scripture is God-breathed — given by His inspiration — and profitable for instruction, for reproof and conviction of sin, for correction of error and discipline in obedience, and for training in righteousness [that is, in holy living, in conformity to God's will in thought, purpose, and action]** (2 Tim. 3:16). When you make a mistake, ask forgiveness and receive it. Thank God for the forgiveness and correction so that you will become a fit vessel for the Master's use.

It is imperative that an intercessor heed sound teaching and . . . **be filled with the full (deep and clear)**

[1]Word Ministries, Inc. (Tulsa: Harrison House, 1989), p. 51.
[2]Word Ministries, Inc. (Tulsa: Harrison House, 1989, 1991), p. 83.

knowledge of His will in all spiritual wisdom [that is, in comprehensive insight into the ways and purposes of God] and in understanding and discernment of spiritual things (Col. 1:9). The intercessor must remain teachable — "growing up in all ways — lovingly expressing truth in all things — speaking truly, dealing truly, and living truly." (Eph. 4:15 KJV, AMP). Do not neglect your study of God's Word. The Holy Spirit will guide you into *all* truth.

Emotion Versus Spirit

Usually there is at least one member in a prayer group who is more emotional than the others. For some unknown reason, people will tend to look upon this one as being very spiritual. They will begin to depend on the emotional reactions of this individual as a sign of the effectiveness of their prayers, or for evidence to determine whether the prayer has been answered or not.

For example, if he or she is crying, that is taken as a sign that more intercession is needed. Laughter might mean that the prayer has been heard and answered.

God does not lead us by our emotions, but by His Spirit: **For as many as are led by the Spirit of God, they are the sons of God** (Rom. 8:14 KJV). His Word is a light unto our path, and a lamp unto our feet. (Ps. 119:105). He leads us by His Word, His peace, and the inner witness: **. . . let the peace (soul harmony which comes) from the Christ rule (act as umpire continually) in your hearts — deciding and settling with finality all questions that arise in your minds . . . .** (Col. 3:15).

The writer of Hebrews asks: **. . . shall we not much rather be in subjection unto the Father of spirits, and live?** (Heb. 12:9 KJV). God is a spirit, and those who worship Him must do so in spirit and in truth. (John 4:24.) In Romans 8:14 Paul gives us insight into how we are to relate to God our Father when he points out that those who are led by the Spirit are the true sons of God. Also, the sixteenth verse of Romans 8 tells us that the Spirit Himself bears witness with our spirit that we are the children of God. So, it appears from these scriptures that God is One Who deals with us Spirit to spirit.

Visions and Voices

Depending on visions and voices apart from the Word of God is dangerous and will lead to spiritual experiences which are not of God. One woman who was being ministered to presented her urgent prayer request concerning two rebellious teenagers who were creating problems in her home. The group immediately went into loud, thunderous, earnest prayer. The answer to the woman's problems was in the scriptures, but no one offered any scriptural basis for the prayer to be prayed or gave instructions on how to pray. After a while she fell on the floor and a young lady, who seemed to be the leader of the group, began to have a vision of a beautiful casket dripping with jewels. As she finished relating her vision, which offered no answer to the problem at hand, everyone became very excited about the vision which had been recounted in very religious terms.

Later, I tried to share the Word of God with the lady who had the problem. She told me that she wasn't interested in what the Bible had to say because she already felt better. How sad, when she went home, she faced the same problems; her situation had not changed at all.

Do not be led astray by voices or visions! God is not "flaky" and does not want His children acting "flaky." Somehow some people have established the idea that to be spiritual one must act weird. *Prayer is a spiritual business, and effective prayers are governed by spiritual laws.* If we adhere to the statutes and teachings of the Bible, people will be drawn to us, not driven away from us.

Fleshly Manifestations

A letter I received from an intercessory prayer group leader described how two women in her group were acting. When a prayer request was shared, one of the women would begin to act like a dog, getting down on her hands and knees, clawing, and scratching. Her friend would then follow her around, "casting out evil spirits," while this woman clawed her legs, even to the point of drawing blood. This practice was driving people away from the group, and the leader did not know how to deal with the situation. Supposedly the one who acted like a dog took on all the evil spirits of the individual for whom the group was interceding. As her friend "cast out the evil spirits from her," it was said to bring deliverance to the person being tormented.

The pastor was unaware of the happenings in this group. I advised this leader to go to the pastor immediately and explain to him what was taking place. These activities were of the flesh (physical manifestations contrived mentally), but applied as if they were spiritually perceived and derived. Later, I received a good report from this church. God had brought them revelation knowledge on prayer through a responsible, effective seminar on intercession.

May God grant that more and more such revelation knowledge and wisdom be forthcoming in the days ahead!

W⁴HO IS CALLED TO PRAY?

A few years ago, after several strenuous days of ministering and taking care of my husband and four children, I walked out of a difficult meeting. I complained loud and long about what I believed to be the root cause of the problem — my intercessors were obviously not doing their job! Had they been, I reasoned, my teaching and ministry would be going much smoother and easier!

When I finally settled down long enough to quit murmuring and complaining, the Lord revealed something to me about prayer. It was during football season, and the Lord used a football game (of all things) to show me how He holds each person responsible for his own personal prayer life.

In the illustration He gave me, I saw that the linemen (the intercessors and those in the ministry of helps) were in position, ready to charge the opposing line and open a path for their backfield to break through. Behind them stood the quarterback (the apostle, prophet, evangelist, pastor or teacher) who was responsible for properly reading the defense and call-

49

ing the right offensive plays. If anyone on the team was out of position or failed to do his job, his actions would affect all the other team members.

Then the Holy Spirit ministered to me that no matter how well the linemen played their positions, since they neither called the plays nor carried the ball, they were very limited in their ability to win the game. Without the well-prepared, mentally alert, physically able-bodied quarterback (the ball handler), theirs was virtually an impossible task. I also realized that the quarterback could not lead his team to victory without the proper preparation and willingness to accept and follow the instructions of his coach.

Once that analogy became clear to me, it didn't take me more than a few seconds to see that I had been wrong in my attitude and actions. I realized that I needed to repent of having laid the blame for my failure on my "teammates" when the real fault was mine for having neglected my duty to spend time conferring directly with my "Divine Coach" and to carefully follow *His* game plan.

The entire Body of Christ, working together in harmony with the Holy Spirit and each other, will produce positive results. Every member of the Body has a place in the Church. Our foundation should be the Word of God; our standard, the banner of love; our clothing, humility.

It is time that we Christians grow into spiritual maturity concerning prayer. Individually, we are parts of one another — mutually dependent upon one another. Jesus did not single out certain individuals to pray. In Luke 18:1, He indicated to us collectively that we . . . **ought always to pray and not to turn coward — faint, lose heart and give up.** Everyone is admonished in 1 Timothy 2:1 to offer petitions, prayers, intercessions and thanksgiving on behalf of all men. Jesus said for us to watch and pray so that we will not enter into temptation. (Matt. 26:41.) That injunction includes everybody!

Successful apostles, prophets, evangelists, pastors and teachers (called by God to fulfill their respective offices) are men and women who maintain an effective prayer life. Ideally, they are surrounded by diverse members of the Body who have answered the call to pray.

We study the lives of many successful people in the ministry, but it is Jesus Who should be our role model for leadership. It is amazing how often we have read the New Testament, seeing the miraculous public ministry of our Lord, but failing to recognize the key to His success. Jesus was a person of prayer; He spent much time fellowshipping with the Father. He spoke what He heard the Father say, and He did what He saw the Father do. Most of those times of prayer and communion were spent in solitude — apart even from His intimate friends and disciples.

In Luke 11:1 we read where Jesus' disciples came to Him and asked Him to teach them to pray. Obviously they recognized that the source of His power emanated from His Father through prayer. So often our prayer time is controlled by needs — usually, desperate needs. Crises, however, never dictated the prayer life of Jesus. He prayed before His times of public ministry and afterwards. The results were evident. We ourselves have heard and seen **how God anointed and consecrated Jesus of Nazareth with the (Holy) Spirit and with strength and ability and power; how He went about doing good and in particular curing all that were harassed and oppressed by [the power of] the devil, for God was with Him** (Acts 10:38). Yet the amazing thing is, Jesus told His followers: **I assure you, most solemnly I tell you, if any one steadfastly believes in Me, he will himself be able to do the things I do; and he will do even greater things than these, because I go to the Father** (John 14:12). Then why are we not yet regularly and systematically producing these ''greater works''? Could the answer be a failure to pray? If so, we are not alone in this fault.

When Jesus prayed, the heavens were opened and the will of God was revealed in every situation as the natural was changed into the supernatural and the Father was glorified. In His hour of greatest need, however, Jesus called three of His closest disciples to accompany Him, requesting that they stay awake and pray. They failed Him — just as we often do.

I know today that to accomplish the work of the Lord we need the prayerful aid and support of others. The cooperation of both leadership and laymen is required. The key to purposeful and powerful ministry is prayer — praying prayers that avail much.

Do intercessory prayer groups have a place in the Church? I believe that they do and that they can be very beneficial in any church in which the pastor is prepared to assume the God-given responsibility of directing the ministry of intercession under the leadership of the Holy Spirit. Today many pastors are personally leading their intercessors in organized prayer, rather than appointing someone else to handle it.

It is necessary that a minister maintain close contact with the prayer group by giving (and receiving) counsel. A group which is led by the pastor himself has direct counsel and knowledge of the specific areas of concern in the church. The mistake which has been made by so many ministers is that of depending solely on the intercessor to hear from God for the direction of the ministry. When this happens, the responsibility for church guidance has been shifted from the pastor to the intercessor. This assignment is not done by God, but by man.

In that case, the intercessor is placed in a position to exercise control over a ministry in a very subtle manner. If that control is allowed to continue, the results can be detrimental to both the ministry and the intercessor. Team members should not make decisions apart from the leadership. If an intercessor accepts the responsibility of hearing from God for a church or other ministry — whether that responsibility is self-imposed or delegated by the pastor — a door is opened for pride to enter the heart of the intercessor.

The Amplified Bible defines pride (''a proud look'') as . . . **the spirit that makes one overestimate himself and underestimate others . . . .** (Prov. 6:17.) There is an established line of authority in the Church, and when it is violated, Satan (who is a shrewd legalist), takes advantage of the situation. Many people desire a position of authority in their church or ministry, but few are prepared or equipped to handle the heavy burden of responsibility that goes with authority. No pastor should relinquish entirely to others his God-given privilege and responsibility of spiritual leadership and determination of God's direction for the church.

Neither should a prayer group attempt to assume the responsibility of the pastor, as happened in a certain local church. In that instance, the intercessors took it upon themselves to hear from God for their pastor. The group began receiving "words" about other members of the church. Forgetting that we are not engaged in warfare against flesh and blood, these people began demanding that the pastor turn certain persons out of the church. These intercessors were good people who loved the Lord and truly wanted to work for Him. But when the pastor wisely refused to comply with their demands, rather than being spiritually mature and allowing God to handle the situation, they became self-righteous in their attitude and actions. The conclusion of the affair was that the intercessors ended up leaving the church, still convinced that they were right. They sincerely believed that since they had "heard from God" in the matter, the pastor was obviously in disobedience to God's will and purpose. They failed to see that they had become dictatorial and overbearing. They had fallen prey to the devil and had unconsciously become guilty of pride — overestimating themselves and underestimating others (namely their pastor and other members of the congregation).

These intercessors were deceived by a familiar (or religious) spirit into believing they were operating in the "discerning of spirits." There is such a thing as the gift of the discerning of spirits. It is referred to in 1 Corinthians 12. But this "gift" operates as the Spirit

of God wills; it never becomes the personal "possession" or prerogative of the individual through whom
it operates. The deception had given way to a critical
and judgmental spirit.

In his book, *Questions and Answers on Spiritual Gifts*,
Howard Carter points out: "There are those who have,
perhaps unconsciously, criticized their brethren, and
have believed they were manifesting this gift [the
discerning of spirits] when they supposedly detected
'demon power' in nearly every meeting they have
entered. They profess to see demon power in the
services, demon influences moving the speaker, demon
spirits everywhere. They have accounted for every lack
of blessing by demon power only, and they have seen
nothing by their supposed exercise of the gift but what
has been bad . . . ."[1]

If your prayer group is only discerning devils, it
is time to seek help. You need to find someone who
can train your members in the art of intercession.
Intercessory prayer must adhere to scripture. Constantly looking for problems and inadequacies in every
situation leads to operating in negativism instead of in
the power of the Holy Spirit. It may be ego-building
to suppose that you know the faults of others through
the discerning of spirits, but the intercessor must be
continually clothed in humility. The purpose of the gift
of the discerning of spirits is "to recognize the presence
of Satan in an individual's life, to deliver him from
Satan's grasp, and to glorify Christ. The gift of discerning of spirits also includes the discerning of angelic

---

[1]Howard Carter (Tulsa: Harrison House, 1976), pp. 97,98.

spirits. God has made angels ministering spirits, many times people discern that an angel is near."[2]

The time has come for the entire Church to answer the call to prayer — those in the five-fold ministry and church members alike. We do not need any more divisions, but instead, harmony and agreement, which will only come about if we pray scripturally as led by the Spirit. In the church at Philippi, there was an occasion for a church split because two women in positions of leadership were of differing opinions. Paul instructed the church to . . . . **help these [two women to keep on co-operating]** . . . . (Phil. 4:3), pointing out that they had toiled along with him in the spreading of the Gospel. We can see the attitude in which Paul prayed, and how he prayed, by looking at the fourth verse of the first chapter of this letter in which he wrote to the Philippians: **In every prayer of mine I always make my entreaty and petition for you all with joy (delight).** As you continue to read the book of Philippians, you will see prayers that Paul prayed for the members while under the inspiration of the Holy Spirit. Here we have an example set before us by one who said, "Follow me as I follow Jesus." (1 Cor. 11:1.) Paul, the apostle, prayed for the churches!

We also find in the sixth chapter of Ephesians that Paul admonished the church at Ephesus to pray. In verses eighteen through twenty he wrote:

Pray at all times — on every occasion, in every season — in the Spirit, with all [manner of] prayer and

---

[2]Rev. and Mrs. J. R. Goodwin, *The Holy Spirit's Three Gifts of Revelation* (Pasadena, Texas: Faith In Depth, Inc., 1974) p. 27.

entreaty. To that end keep alert and watch with strong
purpose and perseverance, interceding in behalf of all
the saints (God's consecrated people).

And also for me, that [freedom of] utterance may
be given me, that I may open my mouth to proclaim
boldly the mystery of the good news [of the Gospel].

For which I am an ambassador in a coupling chain
[in prison. Pray] that I may declare it boldly and
courageously as I ought to do.

The Body of Christ is called to a life of prayer.

Let each of us determine to come into the unity of
the Spirit and faith by praying according to the Word
of God in the spirit. In Matthew 21:13 Jesus noted,
**. . . The Scripture says, My house shall be called a
house of prayer . . . .** Individually, each of us is a temple of the Holy Spirit, or a house of prayer. The many
individuals, or houses, make up one great household
of prayer. Paul sets forth this concept beautifully in
Ephesians 2:20-22:

You are built upon the foundation of the apostles
and prophets with Christ Jesus Himself the chief
Cornerstone.

In Him the whole structure is joined (bound,
welded) together harmoniously; and it continues to
rise (grow, increase) into a holy temple in the Lord —
a sanctuary dedicated, consecrated and sacred to the
presence of the Lord.

In Him — and in fellowship with one another —
you yourselves also are being built up [into this struc-
ture] with the rest, to form a fixed abode (dwelling
place) of God in (by, through) the Spirit.

When each one of us assumes his or her position
on the team or in the army of intercessors, miracles will

begin to take place . . . the plan of God for today will
start to unfold . . . and we will become one in Christ
Jesus so that the world will know that God the Father
has sent His Son for their salvation:

> **For because of Him the whole body (the church,
> in all its various parts closely) joined and firmly knit
> together by the joints and ligaments with which it is
> supplied, when each part [with power adapted to its
> need] is working properly (in all its functions), grows
> to full maturity, building itself up in love.**

> **Ephesians 4:16**

Let each of us assume our God-appointed task in
prayer, giving place to and esteeming our supporting
team members.

5
GUIDELINES FOR INTERCESSION

In 2 Corinthians 10:13-16 there is found a principle for drawing lines of Christian responsibility. In his writings, the Apostle Paul indicates that he will keep within the limits of his commission which God has allotted to him for his measuring line. By this we see that it is not the job of the intercessor to cross lines of scriptural authority by seeking God for direction concerning the operation of another person's ministry.

As an intercessor for a ministry, it is your responsibility to pray for the one who must give an account to God for all ministry decisions. Pray according to the Word of God that the person for whom you are interceding will hear the voice of the Good Shepherd, that the voice of a stranger he will not follow. Directions for the ministry should not be predetermined by the intercessor before the praying begins. Remember, it is to his own Master that the minister will stand or fall, and his Master is able to make him stand. (Rom. 14:4.) Also, remember to pray for specific situations, such as prayer requests and for meetings so that the needs of the people who receive ministry will be met.

If the voice which you hear when you are praying is regularly at odds with the voice of the group leader or minister, you need to find out where the problem lies. Is it that you do not believe in the vision and cannot conscientiously support it, or is the problem caused by the fact that the real motive behind your intercession is a selfish one? Intercessors who feel uncomfortable in situations in which they are not "in the driver's seat," must allow the Holy Spirit to expose the hidden reasons for their discomfort.

If you are one of those persons, ask yourself these questions: Am I looking for personal power and position? Are titles (such as Intercessor or Coordinator of Intercessory Prayer) important to my sense of self-esteem? Am I truly seeking the welfare and benefit of others, or am I really looking for acceptance and recognition for myself?

It is time to speak truly, deal truly, and live truly. Light will dispel the darkness. If a person who is seeking power, position, or recognition refuses to allow the Word of God to expose, analyze, and judge the very thoughts and purposes of his heart, he will find himself operating in manipulation and witchcraft. He will attempt to impose his personal desires upon a ministry or a church, thus usurping the established, God-instituted authority, if possible.

If there is disagreement and disharmony between the spiritual leader and the intercessor, someone has to yield. If agreement cannot be reached, it may be an indication that the person disagreeing with the vision is out of place. From my own experience, I have found that such is often the case. However, it has been evident to me that people who are out of harmony with their spiritual leader and his God-given vision never really find their niche until they allow the Holy Spirit to create within them a steadfast heart. They must be freed of all jealousy and fear by submitting themselves to another person's ministry.

The most dangerous type of intercessor is the individual who must be in control. Persons of this spirit go from church to church, or group to group, believing that they are there to help guide the pastor into the truth. They feel they are sent by God to keep the pastor straight, to correct his theology, and to rearrange his vision. When these persons are asked to step down from their positions, or when they are corrected in some matter, they experience pain and rejection. They still believe that they are right and that everyone else is wrong. They don't realize that by failing (or refusing!) to submit to those in authority, they have brought that pain and rejection upon themselves.

A pastor cannot afford to compromise his vision or to avoid confrontation. Conflicts must be resolved. If problems are not dealt with promptly and decisively, many of God's people will be harmed. If you are called to pray for a ministry, get into agreement with the vision of that ministry and undergird its leader with love, prayer, and faith.

Guidelines for the Pastor

Since most intercessory prayer problems arise in the local church, let's consider the relationship of the pastor to the prayer group. It is the duty of the pastor to pray and receive direction for the church body and

the different church services for which he is responsible. He is the under-shepherd. As such, he is to lead
his people according to the pattern laid down in the
Word of God for all pastors:

> . . . **not by coercion or constraint but willingly;
> not dishonorably motivated by the advantages and
> profits [belonging to the office] but eagerly and
> cheerfully.**
>
> **Not (as arrogant, dictatorial and overbearing
> persons) domineering over those in your charge, but
> being examples — patterns and models of Christian
> living — to the flock (congregation).**

1 Peter 5:2,3

In regard to the intercessory prayer group, the
responsibilities of the pastor are to:

1. Be knowledgeable of intercession by precept and
    practice in order to direct his people in praying all
    manner of prayers.

2. Follow the revealed plan of God — after receiving
    direction from the Chief Shepherd through
    personal prayer — effectively communicating that
    plan to his intercessors.

3. Maintain open communication with the prayer
    leader.

4. Exercise his responsibility of choosing a prayer
    leader who is willing to submit to his leadership
    and to adhere to the church vision: **Now we
    beseech you, brethren, get to know those who
    labor among you — recognize them for what they
    are . . . .** (1 Thess. 5:12).

5. Be careful never to delegate to the prayer group his personal duty and responsibility of praying for the church. The pastor must maintain his God-given leadership role; the prayer group must follow his example — not the other way around.

6. Be willing to listen to the prayer group leader, remembering that he is not looking for a "yes-man," but for a "check and balance" person. When there is a legitimate difference of opinion as to the proper direction of the ministry, the pastor will have to determine whether or not to proceed with the proposed plan. He cannot always wait for everyone involved to see things exactly as he sees them. However, he must continue to keep open communication between himself and his intercessors, praying in accordance with Philippians 3:15: **So let those [of us] who are spiritually mature and full-grown have this mind and hold these convictions, and if in any respect you have a different attitude of mind, God will make that clear to you also.** We can hold different opinions without disagreement and disharmony, if we respect one another. Our goal should be to have the same opinion.

7. Be willing to admit his own mistakes and correct them, asking for forgiveness when necessary, while maintaining his position as under-shepherd of the flock. As a pastor, it is his responsibility to be spiritually and mentally alert, as well as to live a life of self-control so he does not bring reproach to the Gospel.

If you are a pastor, you should be aware that the effectiveness of your public ministry is a direct result of your prayer life. Jesus' prayer life was His key to success; He prayed and the heavens were opened. However, even He desired and sought prayer support, as evidenced by the fact that He asked His disciples to watch and pray with Him during His time of testing in the Garden of Gethsemane. If the Lord Jesus needed prayer support in His trials, then it seems obvious that those of us in the ministry today must develop and rely on the kind of prayerful aid and support which only other concerned believers can provide.

Guidelines for the Intercessory Prayer Leader

An intercessory prayer leader — one who is assigned by the pastor to look after the business and duty of prayer on behalf of the church and to support its God-given vision — must be of good and attested character and repute, full of the Spirit and wisdom of God. (Acts 6:3.)

The leader should be spiritually sensitive to unity within the prayer group. If he sees that there are those in the group who are having difficulty praying in a particular area, he should not pursue that directive for prayer. How can two walk together except they be in agreement? (Amos 3:3.)

It is when we are united in prayer that the power of God is released. It is not the responsibility of the group to pray contrary to the desires of its own members or the decisions of the church leadership. However, all matters of difficulty or disagreement need to be reported to those in authority so they can be resolved.

The prayer group leader must be mature enough to be willing to wait before God and remain teachable. In a multitude of counselors there is safety. (Prov. 24:6.) A God-given leader is one who has learned to recognize and obey spiritual authority.

The duties of the responsible intercessory prayer leader are to:

1. Stay in close contact with the pastor in order to promote harmony and keep prayer within the perimeters of the church vision and the Word of God. At the discretion of the pastor, prayer coordinators may attend church staff meetings and come into the church office for private consultations when needed.

2. Maintain order in the group by setting guidelines according to scriptural principles.

3. Unite the people in the group by setting forth specific areas for prayer.

4. Nurture group members — help them to develop Christian character while being knit together in love.

5. Make and keep members aware that they are a part of a much larger body. The leader must discourage and avoid the development of a clique or secret society. He must keep the door open for new members (intercessors) to join the group.

6. Pray for the needs of group members outside the group prayer time.

7. Be ready to teach on intercession when needed.

Guidelines for a Group Member

A member of an intercessory prayer group must be teachable, willing to yield to reason, a student of God's Word, a worshipper of the true God, and respectful of his assigned leader. If a true intercessor has difficulty with a direction offered by the leader, then it is advisable for the leader to listen, just as it is advisable for the pastor to listen to his intercessors. However, the final decision must remain with the one in charge.

When that person's decision is to overrule the objection and to proceed as he sees fit, this is where the intercessor meets with his first soul-searching test of commitment: ''Has God really called me to pray for this man and this church? If so, am I willing to submit to this established leadership? If I am not willing to submit, is it because I am seeking position or power for myself instead of God's blessing for others?'' Many times, these questions are not easily answered.

A group member must recognize and remember that the group leader is acting in the place of the pastor, and represents an important link in the chain of command set in the church. The motto or slogan of each prayer group member should be the admonishment given all believers in the book of Hebrews: **Obey your spiritual leaders and submit to them . . . .** (Heb. 13:17).

The responsibilities of a group member are to:

1. Lay down his life for the brethren by setting aside the fulfillment of his own personal desires and needs for the sake of others. It is each member's responsibility to pray for his own family in private.

Generally, group intercessory prayer time is for specific prayer for others; therefore, personal prayer requests by individual group members should not be submitted at this time.

2. Be confident and unwavering in his commitment to God, his pastor, his group leader and to the particular church body for which the group is praying.

3. Prepare his heart for prayer ahead of time. Each member must make sure he is free from resentment, unforgiveness, criticism, and judgmentalism. (Matt. 6:12; 7:1.) Each should yield his members as instruments of righteousness unto God.

4. Submit to the leadership and follow the flow of the group spirit under the direction of the leader. No individual member should insist on having his own way. (1 Cor. 13:4-8.)

5. Share, at the appropriate time, what the Holy Spirit has ministered to him personally in given areas of prayer.

6. Be careful not to neglect other areas of ministry in the church. Rather, each member should be a doer of the Word and the work of God. (James 1:22,25.)

7. Spend time with God in praise and worship — apart from the group prayer time.

8. Place a guard over his mouth. The prayer group member must not fall into pride by boasting about the things God is revealing during intercession. The true intercessor is not seeking position, reputation or attention, but is always looking for ways to glorify and serve God the Father. (2 Cor. 10:17.)

Over the years, I have attended many prayer groups. Each one had its own personality. I have seen positive results produced by all different types of prayer activity. We have to ask ourselves how this can be. The only possible answer is that the heart motives of the group are more important to God than outward form or prescribed procedure. We know that God's Word does not return to Him void of power and purpose. When God's people come together with pure hearts, unselfish motives, and faith in Him, believing that He will perform His Word, then their intercessory efforts produce prayers that avail much. (James 5:16.)

Some people enter into prayer with an almost incredible viciousness. They almost seem to reach down, pick up the devil, wrap their arms around his shoulders, and demand a wrestling match with him. They scream, yell, throw karate chops, and launch themselves both physically and emotionally into the fight against what appears to be flying rebel spirits.

There are other groups who pray according to a set pattern, joining their voices together in united prayer. They follow written scriptural prayers, lifting their hearts as one before the Father.

Others pray "together" simply and unpretentiously, but without any set form or order. Quietly and unemotionally, they lift their hearts and voices simultaneously by praying individually in the spirit.

In some instances, the group leader announces the topics for prayer with applicable scriptures as a point of reference. The group members then pray in accordance with the leader as the Holy Spirit leads from one subject to another. Others write all prayer requests on a board and as people file in to the meeting they select subjects for which they feel led to pray.

Some groups pray loudly, some quietly, even silently. There are some whose primary weapon of warfare is praise of the Father or the Trinity. Others begin to moan and groan, preparing themselves for travail.

There are some groups which place great emphasis on physical activity, such as barking like dogs, lying on top of others to impart anointing to them, or staring at pictures or paintings until mesmerized. In my opinion, such activity repels decency and order. In such groups, membership usually becomes selective; only the "elect" or the "elite" of the church can be admitted. This itself is a warning sign.

I have found that prayer groups which function entirely without a leader soon dissolve. This is also true of groups in which everything is "spiritualized" to the point of ignoring practical obligations, such as the preparation of meals and the care of families or homes.

The main problem with prayer group intercession arises when individual groups begin to believe that the way they conduct their prayer service is the (one and only) "correct" manner and that everyone else is wrong. This attitude has been a tool of the enemy to bring intimidation, distrust and disharmony into the Church with the intention of stopping real heart-felt fervent prayer on behalf of the saints.

My position is this: Let each prayer group develop according to the pattern which it believes God has given it. Let each of us follow after the Spirit Who will never cause us to violate the Word of God. Let's covenant to remain teachable and to be willing to conform our own personal or group opinions to the Word of God.

I believe there are scriptural instructions on how to enter into prayer — both privately and corporately. In order to wage successful warfare, a person must know where he is in relation to his commander and his enemy. Likewise, before we can enter into spiritual warfare in prayer and intercession, we first need to locate Jesus, ourselves, and the devil.

Today *Jesus* is physically removed from the surface of the earth. The Apostle Paul tells us:

> . . . **He** (God) **raised Him** (Jesus) **from the dead and seated Him at His [own] right hand in the heavenly [places],**
>
> **Far above all rule and authority and power and dominion, and every name that is named — above every title that can be conferred — not only in this age and in this world, but also in the age and the world which are to come.**
>
> **And He has put all things under His feet and has appointed Him the universal and supreme Head of the church (a headship exercised throughout the church),**
>
> **Which is His body, the fullness of Him Who fills all in all — for in that body lives the full measure of Him Who fills everything everywhere [with Himself].**
>
> **Ephesians 1:20-23**

Physically, *you and I* are here on earth, but spiritually we are positioned in heaven, because . . . **He** (God) **raised us up together with Him** (Christ) **and made us sit down together — giving us joint seating with Him — in the heavenly sphere . . . .** (Eph. 2:6.) *Where?* **Far above all rule and authority and power and**

dominion, and every name that is named — above every title that can be conferred — not only in this age and in this world, but also in the age and the world which are to come (Eph. 1:21).

Some time ago, the Lord graciously gave me a dream which illustrates the location of the *enemy*. In my dream, I walked into my gleaming white kitchen and saw what appeared to be an army of common house roaches advancing toward me. Naturally, I was repelled and began to draw back. Immediately, I became aware that these were no ordinary roaches but vile little creatures with different colored bodies which flashed like neon lights. Spontaneously a strength began to surge up from within me and I thought, "Why, I shouldn't be shrinking back from these ugly little insects; I can step on each one of them and destroy them." With newfound courage, I changed my tactic from retreat to attack. As I advanced toward the loathsome little beasts, they began to run from me. Just then, I woke up.

Immediately upon my awakening, the Holy Spirit reminded me of the words spoken by our Lord Jesus Christ as recorded in Luke 10:19 (KJV): **Behold, I give unto you power to tread on serpents and scorpions, and over all the power of the enemy: and nothing shall by any means hurt you.**

According to Ephesians one, Satan is underneath our feet, because all things have been subordinated to (put under the feet of) Jesus. That means that since we are the Body of Christ here on this earth, Satan and his kingdom of darkness are under *our* feet. The Church of Jesus Christ has been given authority and power over

Satan and his demons. Our enemy is in involuntary subjection to the Church.

Jesus has won the victory. He is the Captain of this great army of saints. He has spoiled the principalities of darkness, making a show of them openly, triumphing over them. (Col. 2:15.)

God has not called you and me to a worrisome, irksome task. He has called us to a life of powerful communion with Him in which we will experience victory and "joy unspeakable." (1 Pet. 1:8.)

Christian, rise up and take your place in this glorious life of intercessory prayer!

6
Hᴏᴡ ᴛᴏ Eɴᴛᴇʀ Iɴ

It has been noted that intercessors sometimes become heavy ladened, overburdened and oppressed. There are those who think that this is the inevitable condition of the true intercessor. Their countenance is sad and they carry their prayer loads for all the world to see. This is not the will of God the Father, but a device of the enemy.

In Philippians 1:4, the Apostle Paul writes: **In every prayer of mine I always make my entreaty and petition for you all with joy (delight).** Intercessors must not become so overwhelmed by the needs of others that simple fellowship with God is neglected. Each and every day we should be in true communion with our Father.

Moses was an intercessor who knew how to enter into this communication with God. The Lord promised that His presence would go with Moses and that He would give him rest. Moses knew that the key to experiencing this rest was spending time alone with God. In order for you to prepare for intercession, you will find it necessary to do as Moses did. Make time every day for communion with your Father — spirit to Spirit.

Psalm 100 gives the outline for entering into the presence of God, which is where true intercession should begin:

First, **Make a joyful noise to the Lord** . . . . (v. 1). Do this regardless of circumstances! Say: "This is the day which the Lord has made; I will rejoice and be glad in it." (Ps. 118:24.)

Second, **Serve the Lord with gladness! Come before His presence with singing!** (v. 2). Begin your time of intercession by delighting yourself in the Lord, for happy is the person whose God is the Lord. (Ps. 144:15.) He requires that those who are His serve Him with gladness of heart. He has supplied fountains of joy within us — He has made us glad! (Ps. 92:4.) Come into His presence with singing, for He has put a new song in our heart. Release it in words and music, **Speak out . . . in psalms and hymns and spiritual songs, . . . making melody with all your heart to the Lord** (Eph. 5:19). Dance before Him, putting off burdens and heavy loads. Make a joyful noise to the Lord!

Third, **Know — perceive, recognize and understand with approval — that the Lord is God! It is He Who has made us, not we ourselves [and we are His]! We are His people and the sheep of His pasture** (v. 3). Exalt the Lord your God. (Ps. 99:5.) The Word is God, and in order to know Him, you must become acquainted with Him through His Word (the Bible) and the Holy Spirit (our Teacher).

Today, so often the work of the enemy is attributed to God by people who have not taken the time to get acquainted with "Our Father which art in heaven." They are unable to "hallow" His Name because they do not know His character.

74

In order to pray effectively, we must know our God. The many different names of God reveal His nature and character.[1] We do not dictate our will to God, but rather we remember that He is the Maker, the Creator, and the Potter. We are His people, and the sheep of His pasture.

Do you know the kind of person you are? Through the positive confession of God's Word, you can begin to see yourself as God sees you. Sometimes it is our mind which is our own worst enemy. We become deceived in areas in which we merely listen to the Word of God, but never obey it. The Word must be applied to our daily living. We must believe what God says about us in His Word.

It is imperative, for instance, that you know who you are — God's handiwork, recreated in Christ Jesus — His very own workmanship. As you pray, you will begin to see yourself and others as God sees His people — the sheep of His pasture. This perspective will build confidence toward God and faith in the ability of God within you to pray effectively.

This, then, is the third step to entering into intercessory prayer — to declare Who God is, and Who He created you to be.

Fourth, **Enter into His gates with thanksgiving and with a thank offering, and into His courts with praise! Be thankful and say so to Him, bless and affectionately praise His name!** (v. 4). Be grateful to the Lord for what He has done and for the things which He has given you. Do not come to the place where you take God and His works for granted. Reiterate His wondrous

---

[1] *Prayers That Avail Much — Volume II,* "ADORATION: 'Hallowed Be Thy Name,' " p. 41.

works and mighty deeds in your life and in the lives of those for whom you intercede. You are responsible for praying for the members of your family. God is looking for an intercessor in each family who will love as Jesus loves, laying down his (or her) life for family members and loved ones.

My mother, Donnis Griffin, as a fifteen year old, paved the way for her entire family (including her parents) to come to the knowledge of the truth. Today her children, grandchildren, and great-grandchildren are all in the Kingdom of God. Since you have answered the call to pray, assume the responsibility of praying for your own family. When praying as part of a group, leave requests for family situations for your own personal prayer times.

In Philippians 4:6, Paul urges: **Do not fret or have any anxiety about anything, but in everything by prayer and petition [definite requests] with thanksgiving continue to make your wants known to God.**

Fifth, **For the Lord is good; His mercy and loving-kindness are everlasting; His faithfulness and truth endure to all generations** (v. 5). Remember this truth and rejoice in it.

The intercessor should not be of a sad countenance, burdened or heavy laden. Jesus said:

> **Come to Me, all you who labor and are heavy-laden and over burdened, and I will cause you to rest — I will ease and relieve and refresh your souls.**
>
> **For My yoke is wholesome (useful, good) — not harsh, hard, sharp or pressing, but comfortable, gracious and pleasant; and My burden is light and easy to be borne.**
>
> **Matthew 11:28,30**

In His presence you are relieved of heavy burdens and set free to become a co-laborer together with God. The intercessor should be the most joyous person on earth. . . . **in Your presence** (Lord) **is fullness of joy, at Your right hand there are pleasures for evermore** (Ps. 16:11). The Holy Spirit will show you the pathway to a life of prayer.

By entering into a time of praise and worship, using Psalm 100 as a model, each person has the opportunity to lay aside thoughts which interfere with . . . **being in full accord and of one harmonious mind and intention** (Phil. 2:2). You have the mind of Christ and hold the thoughts, feelings and purposes of His heart. (1 Cor. 2:16.) In His presence it is easy to **let this same attitude and purpose and [humble] mind be in you which was in Christ Jesus** . . . . (Phil. 2:5).

His purpose is stated in Luke 4:18,19:

> **The Spirit of the Lord [is] upon Me, because He has anointed Me [the Anointed One, the Messiah] to preach the good news (the Gospel) to the poor; He has sent Me to announce release to the captives, and recovery of sight to the blind; to send forth delivered those who are oppressed — who are downtrodden, bruised, crushed and broken down by calamity;**

> **To proclaim the accepted and acceptable year of the Lord — the day when salvation and the free favors of God profusely abound.**

You join with the Lord in His purpose when you pray for the poor, those in captivity, the blind, the oppressed who are downtrodden, bruised, crushed and broken by calamity. Through intercessory prayer, you bring to them salvation and the free favors of God.

Begin to pray for others as the Holy Spirit leads, remembering that He does not lead apart from the Word of God. Learn to hear His voice. Jesus said:

> **I am the good shepherd, and know my sheep, and am known of mine . . . .**
>
> **And a stranger will they not follow, but will flee from him: for they know not the voice of strangers.**
>
> **John 10:14,5 KJV**

There are many voices, many languages. Paul says that none of them is without significance. (1 Cor. 14:10.) Some individuals say that God has never spoken to them, but He has — through the pages of sixty-six books which are bound into two volumes: the Old Testament and the New Testament. God's Word will endure forever.

Know God, know His Word, and pray according to His will. Locate your faith, because when you find God's will on a subject, you must mix faith with what you "hear" (the written Word). You must believe that for which you are praying, and pray with conviction.

Never add to God's will by reading into the scriptures something which they do not say. For instance, you cannot take Psalm 37:4 (**Delight yourself also in the Lord, and He will give you the desires and secret petitions of your heart**) and use it as a basis for asking God for another person's mate or house or car. That would be adding to God's stated will. This manner of praying will produce disastrous results, hurting many people, rather than bringing glory to the Father.

When praying, the motive and intent of the heart must be right before the Lord. In James 4:2,3 the apostle tells his first-century readers:

. . . You do not have because you do not ask.

[Or] you do ask [God for them] and yet fail to receive, because you ask with wrong purpose and evil, selfish motives . . . .

It is imperative that our petitions and intercessions be made out of a heart of selflessness. True intercession is rooted and grounded in *agape* love.

When you are praying God's will for someone, it is not necessary to tell that person about your intercession. Remember, you cannot force anyone to obey God. For example, the husband cannot demand that his wife respect and honor him; neither can the wife demand that her husband love her as Christ loved the Church. It is God Who watches over His Word to perform it. (Jer. 1:12.) Your responsibility is to pray. God will assume His responsibility and bring His words to pass as you apply them through your intercession.

The Word of God says, in order to be saved: **. . . Believe in and on the Lord Jesus Christ — that is, give yourself up to Him, take yourself out of your own keeping, and entrust yourself into His keeping, and you will be saved; [and this applies both to] you and your household as well** (Acts 16:31). Pray without adding anything to God's will; believe and walk in love.

One woman shared how she had prayed almost daily for three years for her alcoholic brother to be saved. She added to God's will by telling God how to perform His Word. After becoming very weary, she asked the Lord what else she could do to receive the answer to her prayers. He told her that it was time for her to believe His promises! It was only a short time after she had begun to believe and have faith in God's

Word that what she had been asking in prayer came to pass. She saw the salvation of God in that situation.

Your prayers for your family will avail much. Never give up — stand, and having done all, stand. (Eph. 6:13.)

Never give up on your local church. Jesus said, **. . . upon this rock I will build my church; and the gates of hell shall not prevail against it** (Matt. 16:18 KJV). A small church in Alabama found itself with only eight members and no pastor. Those eight people discovered God's will for their church, mixed faith with His will, and prayed. Today, two years later, they not only have a pastor, but also have outgrown their building. Many financial miracles have taken place and a community, along with its surrounding area, is coming to know God. When people pray and believe God's Word, He is moved to action on their behalf.

You can be assured that your prayers will avail much when you pray according to God's will, mix faith with your prayers, and walk in love.

> **For as the rain and snow come down from the heavens, and return not there again, but water the earth and make it bring forth and sprout, that it may give seed to the sower and bread to the eater,**
>
> **So shall My word be that goes forth out of My mouth; it shall not return to Me void — without producing any effect, useless — but it shall accomplish that which I please and purpose, and it shall prosper in the thing for which I sent it.**
>
> **Isaiah 55:10,11**

It is my prayer that when Jesus returns, He will find you experiencing the joys of effectual intercessory prayer and will say to you, **Well done, you upright (honorable, admirable) and faithful servant! You have been faithful and trustworthy over a little; I will put you in charge of much. Enter into and share the joy — the delight, the blessedness — which your master [enjoys]** (Matt. 25:21).

7
CHRIST AND HIS CHURCH

Many believers become apprehensive at the thought of what is termed "spiritual warfare." Let me assure you that there is nothing to fear. Certain aspects of the true Church of Jesus Christ provide us with our confidence in His victory for a glorious world in the kingdom, in the air, and in eternity. Initially we need to know about the foundation of the Church and our responsibility in it, and to examine various scriptures which relate to it as the Lord leads us.

"Who Am I?"

When Jesus came into the coasts of Caesarea Philippi, he asked his disciples, saying, Whom do men say that I the Son of man am?

And they said, Some say that thou art John the Baptist: some, Elias; and others, Jeremias, or one of the prophets.

He saith unto them, But whom say ye that I am?

And Simon Peter answered and said, Thou art the Christ, the Son of the living God.

And Jesus answered and said unto him, Blessed art thou, Simon Barjona: for flesh and blood hath not revealed it unto thee, but my Father which is in heaven.

And I say also unto thee, That thou art Peter [a fragment of a rock], and upon this rock [an immovable stone, Christ Jesus Himself] I will build my church; and the gates of hell shall not prevail against it.

Matthew 16:13-18 KJV

Jesus not only promises us that He will build the Church, but He also promises that the gates of hell shall not prevail against it. Which tells me that we Christians are already winners in the face of all opposition to the Gospel of Christ.

Jesus has already set up spiritual warfare so that we are more than conquerors. When He gave His Church the keys to the kingdom, He, in fact, gave the ability, the power, and the authority to overcome all the strategies of the enemy.

In verse 19 Jesus went on to say: **And I will give unto thee the keys of the kingdom of heaven: and whatsoever thou shalt bind on earth shall be bound in heaven: and whatsoever thou shalt loose on earth shall be loosed in heaven.** Binding and loosing is one of the precepts of spiritual warfare. Jesus promised this power to believers.

When you read this entire chapter, you find that Jesus is dealing with prayer and our interdependent relationships with others. Everyone is involved in spiritual warfare, whether he likes to acknowledge it or not. It is all around us; it's ever present — we are all involved.

Jesus, the Son of God

First let's ask, Whom do we say that Jesus is? Isn't it wonderful that through the revelation knowledge that was given to Peter, and also given to us, we can know that Jesus is the Son of the Living God? This Jesus is the Captain of our salvation and He leads us in His triumphant victory over the adversary. The very foundation of our prayer life is based on the question: Whom do we say that Jesus is?

Jesus, the Founder of the Church

The second question is, Who is building the Church? *Jesus!* He said that He would build His Church upon the revelation spoken by Peter — the revelation that "Thou art the Christ, the Son of the Living God." This was a disclosure of Himself, the Rock of Ages.

In verse 18 Jesus said: "Upon this rock I will build My Church." On the day of Pentecost, Peter spoke forth a proclamation of this revelation, bringing deliverance and salvation to three thousand souls. It was Simon Peter who later called Jesus a "living stone" (1 Pet. 2:4 KJV), the "chief corner stone" (v. 6), a "stone of stumbling" and a "rock of offence." (v. 8.) Then, it was Peter who defined believers as "lively stones." (v. 5.)

The Church is built upon the foundation of the apostles and prophets, Jesus Christ Himself being the chief corner stone. (Eph. 2:19-22 KJV.) We are the Church; the Church of Jesus Christ is made up of people whom Peter calls "lively stones."

Lively Stones

The term "lively stones" implies that we are in the process of building something as well as being built into a structure, a dwelling place of God. Jesus has assumed His responsibility in building the Church. He firmly joins and firmly knits us together as each "stone" works properly in all its functions, growing up to full maturity and building up one another in love. (Eph. 4:16.)

Now it is time for us to assume our responsibility as members of the household of faith. Through intercession we repair breaches, restore streets to dwell in, and build up a highway which leads from Satan's domain to life and peace, reconciliation and salvation — the Kingdom of God. (Is. 58:12; Ezek. 22:30.) It was Isaiah who cried, **Go through, go through the gates; prepare the way of the people, cast up, cast up the highway; gather out the stones; lift up a standard or ensign over and for the peoples** (Is. 62:10). Not only are we building highways of deliverance, but we are making up a "wall" by filling up any "gap" which may appear in the wall around those for whom we are praying.

God Himself is our shield; He is our fortress, and He is our fortification; but we are the lively stones that make up the wall and overthrow the plots of the evil one. Jesus is building His house.

Rebuilding the Wall

We turn to the Old Testament for a look at the rebuilding of Jerusalem where worship was restored after the return of the Jews from Babylon. In the Book of Nehemiah, it was the people who built the wall and

God Who fought their battle against their enemies. Even though there was great opposition to the building of the wall round about Jerusalem, it was completed.

It is interesting that when the Israelites began to build the wall, the enemy became very upset; Sanballat was ...**wroth and took great indignation, and mocked the Jews** (Neh. 4:1 KJV) and Tobiah, the Ammonite, declared that even a fox could break down their wall by simply walking on top of it. (v. 3.)

When you and I begin a work for the Kingdom of God, the enemy makes it his business to throw obstacles into our paths. However, we are lively stones with effective weapons of warfare who know the strategies of the devil. Paul tells us that we are not ignorant concerning the devices of the evil one. (2 Cor. 2:11.)

Nehemiah tells us:

> **Those who built the wall and those who bore burdens loaded themselves so that every one worked with one hand and held a weapon with the other hand;**
>
> **And every builder had his sword girded by his side, and so worked. And he who sounded the trumpet was at my side.**
>
> **Nehemiah 4:17,18**

In the New Testament we discover that God through Christ Jesus has fought our battle. Jesus is building His Church; we are co-laborers together with Him; and the Holy Spirit has been sent to aid and bear us up in our inability to produce results. We do not always know which prayer to offer or how to offer it as worthily as we ought. In our inabilities or weaknesses God's strength is made perfect. That which is impossible with man is possible with God. We believers have no reason to be afraid of the enemy for God is on our side. We stand in readiness for the attacks of the enemy, loaded with the armor of God and our sword is the Word of God. (Eph. 6.)

The Holy Spirit knows where the enemy is attacking and gives the trumpet sound — our call to intercessory prayer. Our enemies cannot be seen with the natural eye. You and I are not battling against flesh and blood; we are not praying against people. Our fight is "the good fight of the faith" (1 Tim. 6:12) which takes place in the realm of the spirit. We are in "spiritual warfare" against principalities, against powers, against the rulers of the darkness of this world and wicked spirits in heavenly places.

Reconcilers to Truth

As intercessors we are a vital part of life transformations — reconcilers to truth. We must be aware of the truth which sets us free from all our own destructions. And in order to carry out effective spiritual warfare we must lay aside every weight that would hinder us. If this is to be accomplished we must "speak truly, deal truly, and live truly." (Eph. 4:15.)

Peter defines the approach to this lifestyle in 1 Peter 2:1 of *The Living Bible,* **So get rid of your feelings of hatred. Don't just pretend to be good! Be done with dishonesty and jealousy and talking about others behind their backs.**

It is our responsibility to guard our hearts and recognize that people are not our problem. One of the most successful strategies of the devil is sowing discord among the believers. His objective is to divide and conquer — to set husband against wife, and Christian brother against brother, for example. Therefore, we have to lay aside all malice, all guile, all hypocrisies, envies, and all evil speaking — which empowers us to hold the thoughts, feelings and purposes of God's heart. God has said that His grace is sufficient for us (2 Cor. 12:9 KJV), and it is His grace that enables us to obey the Scriptures.

Speaking, Dealing, and Living Truly

Allowing that we have rationalized our intentions and played mind games with ourselves, we must recognize that it takes the work of the Holy Spirit within us to expose malice and ill-will toward others. A necessary ingredient in spiritual warfare (a truth which I believe cannot be repeated too often) is that we always speak truly, deal truly, and live truly. This does not mean pointing the finger at the other fellow (trying to remove the splinter that is in his eye), but taking moral inventory of ourselves (removing the plank that is in our own eye). We have to make sure our hearts are right; we must put aside all strongholds — all man-made defenses developed during childhood.

It is particularly easy for us to involve ourselves in hypocrisies and spiritual pride, because religious spirits hate intercessors and prayer groups and seek to destroy them. They desire to dominate and control us, causing us to give in to our own systematic rigidity and deception. We must be constantly on guard against a religious spirit causing us to be dogmatic, judgmental, and critical, not leaving room for the weaknesses of other people.

Christian Maturity

Mature Christians should bear the weaknesses of others, keeping their hearts pure, desiring the sincere milk of the Word, that they may grow thereby. (1 Pet. 2:2 KJV.) It is by the Word of God that we mature, being constantly renewed in the spirit of our mind (Rom. 12:2) — having a fresh mental and spiritual attitude which displaces strongholds and man-made defenses that interfere with true intercession.

We are precious in God's Kingdom, and it is our responsibility to walk in that which He has provided for us. He has provided us with both relationship and position. Our relationship with God and man is "servant"; our position is "priest" in a holy priesthood:

If so be ye have tasted that the Lord is gracious.

To whom coming, as unto a living stone, disallowed indeed of men, but chosen of God, and precious,

Ye also, as lively stones, are built up a spiritual house, an holy priesthood, to offer up spiritual sacrifices, acceptable to God by Jesus Christ.

1 Peter 2:3-5 KJV

Therefore, one of the first principles of spiritual warfare is our recognition that we are a holy priesthood, and that our first attention must be given to the praise and worship of our God.

Learn to appropriate the garment of praise to usher you into the place of victorious intercession. Many opposing forces are sent to overcome you and destroy your effectiveness in the Kingdom of God. Praise will stop and still the avenger who has come to deter you and cause you to faint, lose heart, or give up. Preparing for intercession through praise enables you to speak the Word which goes forth like a guided missile and hits its target.

The Garment of Praise

There was a time when I had grown weary in well-doing. It seemed that the very life of God was drained from me. Early one Sunday I was trying to prepare myself for the morning service when the phone rang. It was my mom, saying, "Germaine, do what your church bulletin says to do." I promised her that I would.

Believe me, I did not feel like praying; I did not feel like ministering to anyone; and I certainly did not feel like praising. Very feebly I began to rejoice in the Lord. As I continued I became stronger and stronger. As I began swinging my arms, shouting and dancing all over my kitchen, the spirit of heaviness left and I was clothed in the garment of praise.

You have to have a made-up mind to praise and worship God. The enemy would like to silence you — to keep you quiet: **From the lips of children and infants you have ordained praise because of your enemies, to silence the foe and the avenger** (Ps. 8:2 NIV).

The word *praise* also means "strength." The Psalmist David was not quiet in his praise to his God. Joyous people in the scriptures were not a silent people — they made a joyful noise unto the Rock of their salvation. (Ps. 95:1.) **O clap your hands, all ye people; shout unto God with the voice of triumph** (Ps. 47:1 KJV).

Again and again David admonished the people of his day, Sing praises to God, sing praises: sing praises unto our King, sing praises (Ps. 47:6 KJV). In Psalm 34:1 (KJV) he wrote, **I will bless the Lord at all times: his praise shall continually be in my mouth.**

If you will praise the Lord, the Holy Spirit will give you new songs which you have never heard before. The Holy Spirit, your Teacher will bring New Testament scriptures into focus as you speak to yourself . . . **in psalms and hymns and spiritual songs, singing and making melody in your heart to the Lord** (Eph. 5:19 KJV).

Then, out of the abundance of the heart, the mouth speaks. (Luke 6:45 KJV.) If it's in your heart, it will come out your mouth. Release the glad heart and joyous spirit which God has given you. Make a joyful noise unto God, maintaining the "banks" (worshipping in spirit and in truth), which applies pressure to the rivers of living water, creating the outpouring of the Holy Spirit.

Don't wait to feel like it to begin praising the Lord. Do it because the Bible says to and you will find that you have joined a heavenly host who are praising God in the highest.

Begin your day by proclaiming praises unto your Father: "Father, this is the day that the Lord has made. I will rejoice and be glad in it! That spirit of rejoicing, joy, and laughter is my heritage. I will praise You with joyful lips. I am ever filled and stimulated by the Holy Spirit. Where the Spirit of the Lord is there is liberty — emancipation from bondage, freedom. I walk in that liberty.

"I speak out in psalms and hymns and make melody with all my heart to the Lord. My happy heart is a good medicine and my cheerful mind works healing. The joy of the Lord is my strength. Therefore, I can count it all joy, all strength, when I encounter tests or trials of any sort because I am strong in the Lord and in the power of His might.

"I have the victory in the name of Jesus. Satan is under Jesus' feet. I will not be moved by adverse circumstances."[1]

Most of the time entering into spiritual warfare follows praise and worship to God. (Not always, we can't be dogmatic about these things.) It is the Holy Spirit Who ushers us into the spiritual warfare — as stated earlier, He knows where the next attack will take place.

We must get ourselves into a position to hear from the Holy Spirit Who is always present. I believe that He is constantly attempting to lead us. The reason we have to spend time in praise and worship is so we can quiet our minds and position ourselves to hear what the Holy Spirit is saying.

A Royal Priesthood

You will note in 1 Peter 2:5 (KJV) that the writer tells us that we are a "holy priesthood." Then in verse 9 he calls believers a "royal priesthood." Now, not only do we act to fulfill our position as holy priests unto God, but we also accept our role as royal priests. To

---

[1]Paraphrased excerpt from "To Rejoice in the Lord," *Prayers That Avail Much — Volume I*, p. 35.

do that, we must first understand the function of the high priest in the Old Testament, then look at the priest in the role of intercessor.

Once a year the high priest was permitted to go into the holy place of the temple where he met with God. It was said of Aaron by the Lord in Exodus 28:29 (KJV), ...**Aaron shall bear the names of the children of Israel in the breastplate of judgment upon his heart, when he goeth in unto the holy place, for a memorial before the Lord continually.**

The high priest acted as a mediator — an intercessor — on behalf of the people, appearing before God for them. An intercessor is one who prays for others. The priests were the designated intercessors of the Old Testament. Since you and I belong to this priesthood, we are all empowered to pray and intercede for others.

Priests were constantly reminded of their allotted intercession. The names of the tribes of Israel were engraved on precious stones attached to the ephod and the breastplate which were parts of the priestly robe. The high priest bore the burden of the people upon his shoulders and heart to identify with their need for intercession. His prayers on behalf of the people were his perpetual assignment.

What has God placed upon your heart? It is He Who assigns, Who places "prayer burdens" upon the heart — some for a short period of time, others to be more persistent.

Intercession on behalf of your government, your family, or your church, for instance, is an extended prayer assignment. Sometimes you will find yourself praying regularly for a specific nation or ministry. One lady prays every day for the Jewish people and is acutely interested in reading or viewing anything she finds concerning them. She has already visited the Holy Land, and desires to return to Israel. The names of people or their faces may come before you as a prompting from the Holy Spirit calling you to prayer. At times you will intercede momentarily for someone known or unknown.

Faith Mixed With the Word

One of the quickest ways to sabotage your spiritual warfare is to become confused about the will of God concerning that for which you are praying. Your faith mixed with God's Word will dispel confusion and insure answered prayer: **Wherefore also it is contained in the scripture, Behold, I lay in Sion a chief corner stone, elect, precious: and he that believeth on him shall not be confounded** (1 Pet. 2:6 KJV). To be ''confounded'' is to be confused, and confusion is an enemy to answered prayer.

As long as our faith is based on truth, and our faith is active, we will not become confused. There are many voices out there to distract us. We must know the Word of God and mix our faith with it, knowing that the Father's voice is our surety.

Speaking of the Lord Jesus, Peter tells us:

> **Unto you therefore which believe he is precious: but unto them which be disobedient, the stone which the builders disallowed, the same is made the head of the corner,**

And a stone of stumbling, and a rock of offence, even to them which stumble at the word, being disobedient....

1 Peter 2:7,8 KJV

The disobedient are those who stumble over the Word of God.

Other than the Holy Spirit, the most vital aspect involved in our spiritual warfare is the Word of God. As intercessors, it isn't enough for us just to know the Word. We must be obedient to the Word, not stumbling over it again and again by refusing to obey it. We must live in such a manner that the enemy cannot bring a charge against us.

In truth we are the righteousness of God in Christ Jesus. (2 Cor. 5:21.) It is vital that we know that fact, because it is the prayers of a righteous man that will avail much. (James 5:16 KJV.) We have to know that we have been made the righteousness of God. But when we enter into disobedience by refusing to obey the Word, we leave ourselves open for Satan to bring a charge against us. When we follow after the Spirit, and not after the flesh, who can bring a charge against us? It is God Who justifies, Who puts us into right relation to Himself. (Rom. 8:33.) God does not accuse or impeach those whom He has chosen.

We do not want to leave an opening for Satan's charge, because in spiritual warfare, it is with a pure heart that we enforce the laws of the Spirit of Life in Christ Jesus, reaffirming the devil's defeat. Known sin in one's life strips him of confidence toward God and of the assurance in his divine ability to exercise power and authority over the enemy.

8
WHY SPIRITUAL WARFARE?

We have seen how Nehemiah began to rebuild the walls of the holy city of Jerusalem. We also saw that while the people built the walls, the Lord fought their battles.

Today, just as in Nehemiah's time, the battle is the Lord's. Since that era Jesus has come alive on the pages of history, establishing the overthrow of Satan. If this be true, why do we have to wage any kind of spiritual warfare, and what is the nature of this warfare?

Sometimes wars were fought to obtain certain rights and establish certain laws. Our victory has already been won. God's laws are already on the books. In a sense you and I are like the governing civil authorities who must now enforce these laws of the land. It is our duty to stand against all enemies who would resist and set themselves up in opposition to God's laws. God has delegated to us the power and authority to enforce His divine will in the earth.

The policeman, for example, has delegated power and authority. He is not a terror to people of good conduct, but to those who break the law. Satan and his subjects are the lawless spirits who are constantly trying to overthrow the Kingdom of God. It is this enemy that is terrified of the children of God who know their delegated power and authority — those who understand the power in the name of Jesus.

Satan's reign as the prince of the power of the air is only for a season; he keeps attempting to overthrow the Kingdom of God with guerrilla warfare through deception. Spiritual warfare addresses these enemy forces. In this form of intercession we become the administrators of the victory which was won by our Lord and Savior Jesus Christ when He spoiled principalities and powers, making a show of them openly. (Col. 2:15 KJV.) As spiritual administrators of the triumphant victory of Jesus, we ourselves must avoid disobedience.

A Priesthood Which Has Obtained Mercy

As believers you and I are to God a holy and royal priesthood which has obtained mercy. First Peter 2:9,10 (KJV) tells us:

> **But ye are a chosen generation, a royal priesthood, an holy nation, a peculiar people; that ye should shew forth the praises of him who hath called you out of darkness into his marvellous light:**

> **Which in time past were not a people, but are now the people of God: which had not obtained mercy, but now have obtained mercy.**

We have obtained God's mercy in time of our need. I know that you can look back through your life and see how often the mercy of God was extended to you. You weren't even aware that God was looking out for you.

Because of God's mercy and His grace, we are here today seeking to know more about Him and His workings. Through Jesus you and I have obtained mercy and are admonished to be merciful. Jesus rebuked James and John when they wanted to call down fire from heaven upon a village which would not welcome or receive Him. (Luke 9:53,54.) Isn't this the feeling we have many times when praying for loved ones who do not seem to be responding to the Gospel? God does not want us to call down destruction and calamity on those for whom we pray. Instead, we are to release God's mercy, drawing sinners to Him with bands of love.

Manifesting Mercy and Patience

In the first chapter of the Book of Romans after his characterization of apostates, Paul uttered a profound rebuke which I believe we should heed. It appears to be a plea for the believer to show mercy rather than disdain and contempt for heretics.

Certainly ungodliness is inexcusable and God's judgment is against sin, but He is not against the sinner. God was merciful and patient toward us while we were yet His enemies. (Rom. 5:8.) Now, He is requesting that we manifest that same mercy and patience to others.

Paul writes on this subject:

> "Well," you may be saying, "what terrible people you have been talking about!" But wait a minute! You are just as bad. When you say they are wicked and should be punished, you are talking about yourselves, for you do these very same things. And we know that God, in justice, will punish anyone who does such

things as these. Do you think that God will judge and condemn others for doing them and overlook you when you do them, too? Don't you realize how patient he is being with you? Or don't you care? Can't you see that he has been waiting all this time without punishing you, to give you time to turn from your sin? His kindness is meant to lead you to repentance.

Romans 2:1-4 TLB

In Romans 3, Paul continues to build his dissertation with this statement: **For all have sinned, and come short of the glory of God** (Rom. 3:23 KJV). How can we afford to withhold mercy when we were once blind in our sins and in bondage to the god of this world?

Anyone who responds to the goodness of Jesus can be declared ''not guilty'' — all can be saved in this manner by trusting Him to cleanse them from sin. We can all be justified freely by His grace. In Matthew 5:7 (KJV), Jesus said, **Blessed are the merciful: for they shall obtain mercy.**

It is impossible to pray effectively for those we are yet holding in contempt. Our cry should be, ''Father, forgive them; they know not what they do.'' Release the mercy of God to those for whom you pray — not judgment and condemnation.

Interceding for a Loved One

When I first began to pray for our son's deliverance from the drug scene, I had little understanding about spiritual warfare. I applied the rules governing the prayer of faith to the prayer of intercession.

I had heard that if I prayed more than once for anything, I was praying in doubt and unbelief.

100

However, the Holy Spirit had placed my son David upon my heart and I found myself praying for him again and again. It is possible for a mother's natural love to turn into unforgiveness, but the love of God will sustain her, enabling her to forgive again and again. A parent's emotions run the gamut from feelings of intense love to feelings of overwhelming acrimony. Sometimes her prayers will be very objective — other times filled with fervent, passionate longing to see that child cleansed by the blood of Jesus.

When praying for a loved one, it is imperative that you admit to yourself and the Father the emotional hurts, disappointments, fears, and anger which so often have been denied. Denial of these emotional feelings hinders answered prayer.

There were times when circumstances looked good and I relaxed my intercession for David, only to have to go back and pray him out of adverse circumstances again. In moments of anger I declared that I would never pray for him again, only to find myself drawn once more by the Holy Spirit to a place of spiritual warfare or travail. Such intense intercession is a time for speaking truly and living truly — casting down imaginations and lofty things that seek to exalt themselves above the knowledge of God.

Repeated Intercession

One morning while I was praying I had a vision of a hedge made up of people and angels with flaming swords surrounding David. Yet I still could not understand why the same prayers had to be repeated. It was in the Book of Nehemiah where the Father revealed to me how an addictive person can continually bounce back and forth from compulsive behavior to freedom until he receives emotional wholeness enabling him to overcome toxic addiction.

Remember, your intercession only leads the intercessee to the place of decision; the final decision remains solely with the individual who needs salvation and deliverance.

While Nehemiah was working on the wall, his enemies gathered together, calling him to come down to the plain of Ono and reason with them. But he refused, saying, "I am doing a great work, so I can't come down." (Neh. 6:1-4 KJV.) Nehemiah made a decision which kept him safe.

However, David's reaction to his tempters was quite different. Our prayers did not override David's free will. But when he would go down to the enemy territory, it was the intercession of the saints which would draw him back within the hedge again.

You cannot control the will of another person. You only clear the way for him to hear the Gospel. Sometimes he has to hear it again and again and again before the light of the Truth shines in his heart. The decision is his. During prayer times and afterwards, continue to send forth the Word of God into his life. Strongholds must be pulled down. This is a process that usually does not take place overnight — sometimes it is progressive.

The words that you speak are creative and will not return to God void. Never be moved by good or bad circumstances, but keep your anchor firmly grounded in the Word of God. Remain steady regardless of the situation. Don't give up your position of priesthood or abort the mission which God has placed on your heart. You will know through the witness of the Holy Spirit when you have fulfilled your assignment. There will be a definite release within you — a knowing that must be experienced personally in order to be completely understood. Pray, extending forgiveness, obtaining mercy and grace, until the work is accomplished.

A Burden for Prayer

I well remember an incident from my teenage years which reveals a temporary "burden" for prayer.

Our family had gone to visit my grandparents and we were returning home when we had a brush with death. The next day one of the church members called my dad to inquire if our lives had been in danger at a certain moment. He said that about that time God had awakened him, and our faces had flashed before him as he interceded in the Spirit.

In this case, the Father found someone who responded to His call, someone who was faithful to pray, protecting us from an accident which could have snuffed out our lives. This man fulfilled his role as a priest unto God on behalf of his pastor and his family in a time of crisis.

God wants your prayer time devoted to situations outside of your own personal problems. Develop the mind of Christ within you, holding the thoughts, feelings, and purposes of His heart. (Phil. 2:5 KJV.)

A Sweet-Smelling Fragrance

The tabernacle, in the Old Testament temple worship, was the altar of incense which was placed before the ark of the testimony. Incense was burned upon the altar morning and evening. It was symbolic of acceptable prayers.

In the New Testament this altar is now placed just before the throne of God. When you come before God, you come into His throne room, presenting yourself before His throne. Your prayers are a sweet-smelling fragrance before God. They are a perpetual and continual flow before the Lord, because prayer is persevering. Jesus said to pray without ceasing. Every prayer that you have ever prayed is in the throne room as incense before the Lord.

Broaden Your Vision

The Holy Spirit desires to broaden the scope of your prayer life. The Father has a plan for mankind and He desires that you become involved in that plan. He wants you to expand your prayer borders beyond the confines of your home and your local church. (However, do not neglect these vital areas of prayer.)

In Psalm 2:8 (KJV) the Father said: **Ask of me, and I shall give thee the heathen for thine inheritance, and the uttermost parts of the earth for thy possession.** Broaden your vision. Allow the Lord to imprint His intercession on the tablets of your heart — delegating prayer assignments to you as He wills. He wants you to become Kingdom-minded in preparation for the return of Jesus. Expand your prayer vision to include nations. Get beyond the needs of your family as well as those prayer situations in the local church.

Remember, these problems originate in the spiritual realm and affect the soul, resulting in various forms of behavior. Pray for the will of God to be done on earth as it is in heaven. Problems should not dictate your prayer life. You should be led by the Spirit of God, carrying out His prayer assignments. Whether it is for the family, the church, the community, or the nation, remain faithful to your assigned prayer burden until it is fulfilled.

Agree With the Plans and Purposes of God

Involve yourself in the things which Jesus is doing. You were destined from the beginning to be molded into the image of God's Son. (Rom. 8:29.) Act like Jesus. Walk like Jesus. Talk like Jesus. Adopt the same attitude and purpose which was in Christ Jesus. (Phil. 2:5.) In His present-day ministry, Jesus is the High Priest Who intercedes before the Father-God:

> **Seeing then that we have a great high priest, that is passed into the heavens, Jesus the Son of God, let us hold fast our profession.**
>
> **Hebrews 4:14 KJV**

In Greek the word translated profession is *homologia*, which means, "agreement; terms of surrender[1]; confession[2]." Let us meet the terms of surrender to God by affirming our faith in Him and His Word. This requires agreement with the plans and purposes of God.

---

[1]James Strong, *The Exhaustive Concordance of the Bible* (Nashville: Abingdon, 1890), "Greek Dictionary of the New Testament," p. 53, #3671.

[2]Finis Jennings Dake, ed.; *Dake's Annotated Reference Bible* (Dake Bible Sales, Inc., P. O. Box 625, Lawrenceville, GA 30246, 1963); p. 246 of New Testament, Col. 1, note "K."

For we have not an high priest which cannot be touched with the feeling of our infirmities; but was in all points tempted like as we are, yet without sin.

Hebrews 4:15 KJV

According to W.E. Vine, *infirmities* means "want of strength,...weakness,...inability to produce results...."[1]

Many times in prayer we experience an inability to produce results, but Jesus is touched with these infirmities. According to Matthew 8:17 He bore these weaknesses and in Romans 8:26 we find that He and the Father sent a Helper Who takes hold together with us against these inabilities in order to produce results. Jesus has made us "kings and priests" unto God the Father. (Rev. 1:6 KJV.)

As New Covenant believers you and I are part of "an holy priesthood" (offering up spiritual sacrifices, acceptable to God by Jesus Christ) and "a royal priesthood" (that we should show forth the praises of Him Who has called us out of darkness into His marvelous light). (1 Pet. 2:5,9 KJV.) The first ministry of a New Testament priest is to offer up praises to God; the second is to declare His wonderful salvation through a life which emulates Jesus.

When we who are priests under the New Covenant pray here on earth, our High Priest presents our petitions before the Father.

A Successful Prayer Life

Examination of the lives of prominent Christian men and women reveals that they were, and are, men

---

[1]*Vine's Expository Dictionary of New and Old Testament Words* (Old Tappan: Fleming H. Revell, 1981), Volume 2: E-Li, p. 257.

and women of prayer. Jesus has given us believers a pattern for successful living which includes a successful prayer life.

In the Song of Solomon 2:13,14 a superb passage of scripture calls us into a wonderful relationship to our Lord. The bridegroom (representing Christ) is saying to his beloved bride:

> . . . Arise, my love, my fair one, and come away.

> . . . let me see your face, let me hear your voice, for your voice is sweet and your face is lovely.

This is the call of Jesus to the Church today: "Arise, come apart, come away with Me." Everyone who spends time with Jesus discovers divine plans and purposes for his life: **The Lord confides in those who fear him; he makes his covenant known to them** (Ps. 25:14 NIV). What has God placed on your heart? The Christian's prayer armor is of the spirit and God has written certain prayer ventures on your breastplate.

A sincere desire to have a successful prayer life necessitates looking beyond situations, problems, and circumstances. Don't be afraid of prayer burdens. Jesus said, . . . **my yoke is easy, and my burden is light** (Matt. 11:30 KJV). Paul wrote:

> For our light affliction, which is but for a moment, worketh for us a far more exceeding and eternal weight of glory;

> While we look not at the things which are seen, but at the things which are not seen: for the things which are seen are temporal; but the things which are not seen are eternal.
>
> **2 Corinthians 4:17,18 KJV**

Situations in this world in which we live in the flesh are constantly changing, but the things of the Spirit are unchanging. Involve yourself with the intercession of Jesus. Become utterly one with Him.

Jesus, Our Foundation

God has said that His house would be called a house of prayer. (Is. 56:7; Matt. 21:13 KJV.) You and I are that habitation with a firm and sure foundation. In 1 Corinthians 3:11 we find that no man can lay a foundation other than the one which is laid, Jesus Christ. So, as our Foundation and High Priest, Jesus is our backing for all prayer including spiritual warfare.

The Church was a mystery in the Old Testament, but today we are the Church. Isaiah prophesied about the Church when he said:

> **Therefore thus saith the Lord God,**
>
> **"Behold, I am laying in Zion a stone, a tested stone,**
>
> **"A costly cornerstone, for the foundation, firmly placed."**
>
> **Isaiah 28:16 NAS**

Jesus, our Foundation and Builder, says, "The gates of hell shall not prevail against you." (Matt. 16:18 KJV.) Hallelujah! Because of this truth, we know that spiritual warfare is not something to be feared.

You are ready to assume your responsibility in the household of faith, knowing that you are a winner — more than a conqueror — called to a life of intercession. You belong to a holy and royal priesthood.

9
PRACTICAL SPIRITUAL WARFARE

Is it possible to look at spiritual warfare in a practical manner? I believe that it is since there are principles and guidelines which we can unveil in the Scriptures.

Spiritual warfare is not mystical or eerie. God Himself is practical in His instructions for living the more abundant life, which includes communication with the Trinity via prayer. He has not left us to wander aimlessly around, hoping to stumble onto proper prayer techniques. He is a loving Father Who knows how to reveal His ways to those who will abide in His presence.

Assuredly there is a warfare spoken of in the Bible. Everyone is called to a ministry of reconciliation — a warfare against sin and Satan. Therefore, whether we acknowledge it or not, every believer is in spiritual warfare. To wage this fight, which Paul calls a ''good warfare'' in 1 Timothy 1:18 (KJV), each one must cling tightly to his faith in God's Word and maintain a clear conscience.

Spiritual Weapons

Again Paul speaks of this warfare in 2 Corinthians 10:3,4 (NIV): **For though we live in the world, we do not wage war as the world does. The weapons we fight with are not the weapons of the world. On the contrary, they have divine power to demolish strongholds....**

These spiritual weapons are for the destruction of enemy strongholds — reasonings programmed by philosophy, religious dogmas, childish suppositions, and ideas fashioned after and adapted to this world's external, superficial customs. These proud arguments and obstacles are fortifications which have set themselves up against the knowledge of God.

The true intercessor refuses to be conformed to this world, but is transformed by the renewing of his mind, that he ...**may prove what is that good, and acceptable, and perfect, will of God** (Rom. 12:2 KJV). This is required if we truly present our bodies as living sacrifices unto God, which is our reasonable service and worship. (Rom. 12:1 KJV.)

Building Up Through Worship

It is imperative that we keep ourselves built up through worship. God is looking for true worshippers — those who will worship Him in spirit and in truth. (John 4:24 KJV.) Worship keeps us secure in the secret place of the Most High:

> **A thousand may fall at your side, and ten thousand at your right hand, but it shall not come near you.**

> Only a spectator shall you be [yourself inaccessible in the secret place of the Most High] as you witness the reward of the wicked.
>
> Because you have made the Lord your refuge, and the Most High your dwelling place,
>
> There shall no evil befall you, nor any plague or calamity come near your tent.

> **Psalm 91:7-10**

You do not have to be afraid of the enemy's tactics. Continually throughout the Word of God we read, "Do not fear," "Be not afraid," "Be of good courage." You do not have to fear that demons will jump on you or attach themselves to you. Fear opens the door for demonic activity; faith is your shield that will . . . **quench all the flaming missiles of the wicked [one]** (Eph. 6:16). You are inaccessible in the secret place of the Most High.

Praise and worship will usher you into intercession. Maintain an attitude of worship by acknowledging the presence of God at all times. His praise is to be continually in your mouth.

Recognize the Enemy

In practical warfare one must recognize his enemy.

There was a time when I treated my husband as though he were my enemy. Before I learned to pray prayers that avail much, as I mentioned before, I tried every tactic that I knew to force him to go to church. After all, this was certainly the will of God. He needed to be a good example to our children and, besides that, I was tired of always feeling so alone.

111

Every Sunday morning the battleground was set. I woke up the children, fed them breakfast, and saw that they got dressed properly, while my husband remained in bed. At every opportunity I ran to the bedroom nagging, coercing, speaking gently, screaming, among other things. Sometimes I would wake the children early and send them into the bedroom to wake Daddy.

One day the Holy Spirit said to me, "Since you have prayed, believe." The gentle voice of the Spirit instructed me to treat my husband just as I would if he were attending church. I realized that believing is acting as though God has heard and answered prayer. This is action added to faith.

Sunday mornings were certainly easier for me and the children once I changed my behavior through the grace given me by the Lord Jesus. My prayers began to avail much as I prayed according to the will of God, no longer wrestling against my husband, but against spiritual rebels. It was only a few weeks later that I walked into the living room and saw my husband dressed, announcing that he was going to church with us.

Everette was not my enemy. The situation had to be attacked in the spiritual realm where strongholds had been set to prevent him from obeying God. It is God Who receives all the glory, praise and honor. I did only the possible; He did the impossible.

The Devices of Satan

Ephesians 6:10-18, which describes our prayer armor and lists our weapons of warfare, exposes the enemy and his ranks. Paul begins in verse 10 by giving believers an exhortation to develop and exercise courage in spiritual warfare against the enemies of God.

These unseen enemies are trying to turn us from the Lord; to create fear, doubt, and unbelief; to induce us to be unfaithful to God's Word. Satan uses deceit, pressure, and cunning craftiness as snares set to keep our attention on problems, provoking us to believe that other people are to blame for our circumstances. He then succeeds in disguising the root cause of the problem, which is found in the spiritual realm.

Satan sends us thoughts of accusation against people in an attempt to create a proud look, a lying tongue, hands that shed innocent blood, a heart that devises wicked imaginations, feet that are quick to rush into evil, and a false witness that speaks lies. He wants his activities to be camouflaged while we hurl accusations at one another, sowing discord among the brethren.

Satan's greatest delight is to disturb harmony. Another favorite ploy is heaping condemnation on the believer, turning him against himself. Paul makes it clear that we are not to be against one another or ourselves, but against spiritual rebels.

Wrestling Against Spiritual Enemies

Finally, my brethren, be strong in the Lord, and in the power of his might.

Put on the whole armour of God, that ye may be able to stand against the wiles of the devil.

For we wrestle not against flesh and blood, but against principalities, against powers, against the rulers of the darkness of this world, against spiritual wickedness in high places.

Ephesians 6:10-12 KJV

113

Jesus knew that there would be people who would not accept us, but who would set themselves against the Word of God which we preach. Yet He said to us, **. . . Love your enemies, bless them that curse you, do good to them that hate you, and pray for them which despitefully use you, and persecute you** (Matt. 5:44 KJV). Our Lord was never against people, only against the evil one who holds people in bondage.

Paul's writings are in harmony with the teachings of Jesus. Here in Ephesians he says that we are not to wrestle against people, or to set ourselves against them, but that our battle is against Satan. So, what is the practical application of this scripture? How does one wrestle with the devil?

One day while searching for the true meaning of this word *wrestle* in Vine's expository dictionary I came across two seemingly insignificant shades of meaning: "sway" and "vibrate." Mr. Vine wrote that ". . . wrestling. . . is used figuratively, in Eph. 6:12, of the spiritual conflict engaged in by believers."[1]

The two synonyms given made no sense to me. I tried out, "We *sway* not against flesh and blood," then, "We *vibrate* not against flesh and blood." It appeared that these two words simply did not work in that context.

When I would call up a mental image of the word *wrestle*, my mind would immediately present a picture of two massive men in various holds, each trying to pin the other for the count of three. I realized that if

---

[1] W.E. Vine, *Vine's Expository Dictionary of Old and New Testament Words* (Old Tappan: Fleming H. Revell, 1981), Volume 4: Set-Z, p. 239.

Jesus had not defeated Satan, I would have been in big trouble. Somehow I could not see myself in this kind of struggle with the devil.

However, mental images of the words *sway* and *vibrate* didn't bring any acceptable revelation. I knew that scripture must interpret scripture. The only swaying I could think of that would appear scriptural was that of the trees planted by the rivers of living waters in Psalm 1, which could be a representation of believers as they were buffeted by the storms and winds. That seemed pretty good — it illustrated the fact that we cannot be uprooted. But somehow I knew that there was more to be understood.

The word *sway* has both a positive and a negative meaning. According to Webster's dictionary it means "to swing or move from side to side, or to and fro — to vacillate or alternate between one position or opinion and another." Some believers try to function in this mind set, swaying back and forth between different kinds of teaching, or being "double minded" as James called it (James 1:8), and thus receiving nothing from God. They grow weary in their prayer life and many of them faint in their minds.

However, there is another meaning of this word *sway*. It also means "to rule, to reign, to hold sway; to cause a person, an opinion or actions to be inclined a certain way or be turned from a given course or diverted." Therefore to *sway* means "to rule over, control, dominate or prevail."

According to Ephesians 1:20-22, we believers are seated in heavenly places in Christ *far above* the earthly realm. Yes, there is spiritual warfare going on all around us, but we hold sway over Satan and his forces. In the name of Jesus, we have the authority, power, might, and strength to cause Satan to turn from a given course.

Isn't that what we are trying to do in spiritual warfare — to turn the course of Satan, to divert him from that which he has plotted and planned against the Body of Christ? In spiritual warfare we hold sway over him, not over human beings; we have authority and control over principalities, powers, the rulers of the darkness of this world, and spiritual wickedness in heavenly places.

In one place the psalmist said, ''It's as though we were dreaming.'' (Ps. 126:1.) It is almost too good to be true, but you and I have power and authority over the evil one.

Church, let's awaken, stop our moaning and groaning about the wiles of the devil, and assume our place of spiritual authority, behaving like sons and daughters of the Most High God.

Vibrating Light or Wavering Opinion?

What about the word *vibrate?* According to Webster it means ''to give off light or sound by vibration.'' A vibration is an emotional quality or supernatural emanation that is sensed by another person or thing.

The world talks about walking into a room and sensing ''vibes.'' I know that havoc must take place in the seat of Satan's empire as we believers stand clothed in the armor of light, praying all manner of prayer. Light dispels darkness: **And the Light shines on in the** darkness, for the darkness has never overpowered it — put it out, or has not absorbed it, has not appropriated it, and is unreceptive to it (John 1:5). Jesus said to His disciples, **Ye are the light of the world...**(Matt. 5:14 KJV). Paul wrote, **For once you were darkness, but now you are light in the Lord; walk as children of light...**(Eph. 5:8).

The negative meaning of *vibrate* is "to vacillate or waver as between two opinions" (i.e., between belief and doubt, faith and fear). This frustrates the purposes and plans of spiritual warfare. Swaying or vacillating between two opinions is the result of the presence of strongholds which have not yet been pulled down: **...the weapons of our warfare are not carnal, but mighty through God to the pulling down of strong holds** (2 Cor. 10:4 KJV).

How do we "sway" and "vibrate" against spiritual rebels? By putting on the whole armor of God and praying at all times — on every occasion, in every season — in the Spirit, with all [manner of] prayer and entreaty. (Eph. 6:18.) By speaking God's Word, praying with the understanding. God's Word is our sword, and when the enemy comes to destroy our homes, churches, and communities, we defeat him by affirming God's Word over everything that concerns us.

The entrance of God's Word brings light, dispelling darkness. (Ps. 119:130.) When Jesus was confronted by Satan, He declared, "It is written," quoting from the Old Testament scriptures. (Luke 4.) Turn to the Word of God for answers. Affirm the Word in your meditation and through prayer. There is no better prayer book. God is watching over His Word to perform it. (Jer. 1:12.)

10
THE OVERTHROW OF SATAN

It is evident that Satan is still at work to deceive, accuse, divide, and overthrow the Church of the Lord Jesus Christ. The Church is a sleeping giant awakening to the truth of the utter defeat of Satan.

Jesus spoiled principalities and powers, making a show of them openly — exposing Satan to public shame. (Col. 2:15 KJV.) In Genesis 3:15 KJV the Lord revealed that the enemy would "bruise the heel" (a metaphor for temporary suffering) of the Seed of the woman, while promising that the Seed was to utterly crush and eternally defeat Satan. Little did Satan know that the death of Jesus would be his absolute defeat.

It is imperative in successful spiritual warfare that we understand the victory that was fought and won by our Redeemer Who conquered Satan by dying for us. In Colossians 2:15 (NIV), Paul reveals the absolute defeat of the devil by Jesus Christ, **And having disarmed the powers and authorities, he made a public spectacle of them, triumphing over them by the cross.**

Now, God, through Christ Jesus, through the cross, has already disarmed principalities and powers. In 1 Corinthians, the second chapter, we find that had the prince of this world known what was going to happen, he would never have crucified the Son of God. In that crucifixion came his defeat.

The Location of Jesus

Paul then receives the divine revelation of how Jesus utterly defeated Satan, his principalities and powers. We have shared in an earlier chapter our relation to our Commander-in-Chief and our enemy. Again we will locate Jesus, Satan, and believers — the Church. We need to have an understanding of where we are all located in the spirit realm in order to carry on strategic warfare. We will locate Jesus first.

In Ephesians 1:20-22 (NIV) we find Paul referring to the power of God...

> **which he exerted in Christ when he raised him from the dead and seated him at his right hand in the heavenly realms** (where?),
>
> **far above all rule and authority, power and dominion, and every title that can be given, not only in the present age but also in the one to come.**
>
> **And God placed all things under his feet and appointed him to be head over everything for the church, which is his body, the fullness of him who fills everything in every way.**

The physical location of the Lord Jesus today is at the right hand of the Father, where He sits in glory as the spiritual Head of the Church.

Location of the Church

It is also vital that we understand our spiritual location as we approach spiritual warfare. In Ephesians 2, we find that we were once children of disobedience, objects of wrath, under the control of the prince of the power of the air (Satan). We were powerless to deliver ourselves from this bondage. But God, Who is rich in mercy, made us alive with Christ, raised us up with Him, and seated us with Him in the heavenly realms. (Eph. 2:4-6 KJV.) So, where are we located? *In Christ!* Where is that? If we are truly in Him then we are seated *far above* all principality, and power, and might, and dominion, and every name that is named not only in this world, but also in that which is to come.

This elevated status does not put us in a position to lord it over people but in a position to be the delegated authority in the world of the spirit. It appears to me that we already hold the keys to victory; we already have the victory since we are already seated with Christ in heavenly places. That means that Satan is somewhere out there, and when we get him located, we find that he is underneath the feet of Jesus — a defeated foe.

It seems almost too good to be true when we begin to comprehend the position of the Body of Christ — the Church. Often our mental image has been one that suggests that Satan is just barely under our feet and we are actually treading on him. This is not the picture we get from Ephesians where we find that we are seated far *above* the satanic regime.

Our Lord won a decisive battle — not just a skirmish that gives us limited authority over the enemy, but a *total victory* that renders the devil paralyzed. (Heb. 2:14,15.)

Even before the death and resurrection of Jesus, He sent His disciples out, saying, **Behold! I have given you authority and power to trample upon serpents and scorpions, and (physical and mental strength and ability) over all the power that the enemy [possesses], and nothing shall in any way harm you** (Luke 10:19).

Jesus gave physical and mental strength and ability to carry out the work which He had begun while here on earth. Jesus went about in towns and villages teaching in synagogues and preaching the Good News of the Kingdom and healing every disease and every weakness and infirmity among the people. (Matt. 4:24.) Then in John 14:12 (NIV) He said to His disciples, **"I tell you the truth, anyone who has faith in me will do what I have been doing. He will do even greater things than these, because I am going to the Father."**

You and I are to do the works of Jesus, knowing that the prayers of a righteous man avail much. Jesus knew that there would be opposition to the Gospel and that His people would suffer persecution, but He wants you and me to know that the defeat of Satan was effective and we are to keep it in effect.

The Location of Satan

Even before His death, burial, and resurrection Jesus gave His disciples power over the enemy in His name. Are we to suppose that now, after the resurrection, the Church has less power than these men had before the cross? Never! How dare we continue to glorify the works of the devil with our proclamations and testimonies and, in some cases, our fears.

Satan is a defeated foe.

The prophet Isaiah says that we will look at Satan and say, ''You mean this is the man who shook the earth and made kingdoms tremble?'' (Is. 14:16.) When we realize that Satan's power and authority over the Church of the Lord Jesus have really been broken and put to naught, we will begin to be even more effective in our prayers.

We can see from the passage in Luke that Satan does not have authority over the children of God. His only weapon is deception through fear. Let's change our focus from the works of Satan to the wondrous works of God.

Great things He has done!

It was Nehemiah who said to the people of his day: ''Don't be afraid; the Lord will fight your battles.'' (Neh. 4.) If the Lord would do that for those under the Old Covenant, how much more would He desire to do that for us who are under the New Covenant? Not because He cares for us more than He cared for ancient Israel, whom He called the apple of His eye, but because of what was accomplished through the cross.

Hebrews 2:14,15 (NIV) is an exciting bold statement about Jesus Christ: **Since the children have flesh and blood, he too shared in their humanity so that by his death he might destroy him who holds the power of death — that is, the devil — and free those who all their lives were held in slavery by their fear of death.**

Jesus has made Satan of no effect, has brought him to naught. Jesus paid a debt He did not owe. We could not get out of our bondage, but Jesus came on our behalf. He dealt a fatal blow to Satan that made Him of no effect, and delivered us out of bondage. That which was impossible with man was possible with God.

Satan works through deceit, through confusion of the minds of people. In order to pursue his destruction in the earth, he has to get human cooperation. To accomplish his earthly deeds, he needs physical bodies.

Sin begins with a thought. (James 1:14.) Where does discord begin in our homes and churches? It begins with a thought. When that thought is considered valid, we begin a progressive search to prove its validity. Thoughts against others; feelings of rejection, intimidation, insecurity; belief that others are against us; high-minded attitudes which convince us that we are better than others, causing us to overestimate ourselves and underestimate others — all such mental activity is contrary to truth. The next thing we know we are speaking out what we are thinking, and those words begin to build fires among our co-workers, friends, and companions. Then everything gets out of hand and we can't imagine how it all began. The result of wrong thinking is strife and every evil work.

Responsibility in the Church

Division is in the church, the home, the community, and the office. Brother against brother; pastor against his congregation ("If only they would straighten up and quit gossiping about me..."); congregation against pastor ("If only he would behave...").

Strife and discord affect everyone.

What is our responsibility as the Body of Christ, those "lively stones" about which Peter wrote? As living stones we have a part to play in the Church of Jesus Christ. God did not create passive stones, He created lively stones. We are to exercise all the power that He has given us in the spirit realm. Our heavenly Father has given us power to be creative in this world, to exert a positive influence, to make a difference in the cities and towns in which we are planted.

All of us are to make a difference in our churches, in our neighborhoods, and in our businesses and homes. I want to remind you once again that Jesus said that the gates of hell shall not prevail against us. Sometimes it looks as if God has got a lot to do to make that statement come true. Sometimes it looks as if the gates of hell are prevailing. That is when our faith comes into the picture. By faith we reach out and take hold of what Jesus said, "The gates of hell shall not prevail against *you*!"

11
LIFE IN THE PRAYER CLOSET AND BEYOND

Now that your foundation and prayer responsibility as a priest have been established, let's look at prayer as a lifestyle both in the prayer closet and beyond.

In Matthew 6, Jesus spoke to His disciples about prayer, saying:

> "But when you pray, do not be like the hypocrites, for they love to pray standing in the synagogues and on the street corners to be seen by men. I tell you the truth, they have received their reward in full. When you pray, go into your room, close the door and pray to your Father, who is unseen. Then your Father, who sees what is done in secret, will reward you. And when you pray, do not keep on babbling like pagans, for they think they will be heard because of their many words. Do not be like them, for your Father knows what you need before you ask him."

Matthew 6:5-8 NIV

Then in verses 9 through 13 Jesus gives us a prayer outline, commonly known as the Lord's Prayer. He continues His teaching on prayer with these words:

"For if you forgive men when they sin against you, your heavenly Father will also forgive you. But if you do not forgive men their sins, your Father will not forgive your sins."

Matthew 6:14,15 NIV

Jesus here connects prayer and forgiveness, an essential ingredient in the development of healthy relationships. Prayer enables us to pull down strongholds which prohibit unity in private households as well as in the household of God.

Major Strongholds

Paul tells us that **...the weapons of our warfare are not carnal, but mighty through God to the pulling down of strong holds** (2 Cor. 10:4 KJV). Strongholds, places of security or survival, are established in the mind. Many of these were developed during childhood as defenses against imaginary or actual dangerous emotional or physical situations. Even though our perceptions of events which took place may have been perverted and distorted, the strongholds are real. If carried over into adulthood, they sabotage what could be good, healthy relationships.

The tragedy is that past hurts and disappointments so often lead to unforgiveness, which is the greatest hindrance to answered prayer. Jesus spent most of His ministry preaching about the logistics of human relationships. He told His followers, **And whenever you stand praying, if you have anything against any one, forgive him and let it drop — leave it, let it go — in order that your Father Who is in**

heaven may also forgive you your [own] failings and shortcomings and let them drop (Mark 11:25).

I know that you have experienced those times when you have talked with someone who could neither hear nor understand what you were saying. Later you discovered that you had not heard the other person accurately either. You have come up against a stronghold or mind set. These strongholds interfere with the voice of the Holy Spirit and divert us from the purpose and will of God in our prayer life, causing us to pray according to our wishes. We do not hear what the Spirit is saying; we do not understand His direction.

If your heart is truly after the things of God, then the Holy Spirit does not give up on you. He sends you the Truth that enables you to pull down every stronghold, **Casting down imaginations, and every high thing that exalteth itself against the knowledge of God...** (2 Cor. 10:5 KJV).

The enemy's strongholds are ignorance, prejudices, lusts, imaginations, carnal reasonings, and pride. (1 John 2:16.) Our prayers must be according to the will of God, not according to imaginations and unhealthy mind sets based on "doing our own thing," or instant gratification of our material desires.

Life Beyond the Prayer Closet

Life in the prayer closet can insure a successful life beyond the prayer closet. God is interested in His children developing healthy relationships, for then we can ...**give attentive, continuous care to watching over one another, studying how we may stir up (stimulate and incite) to love and helpful deeds and noble activities** (Heb. 10:24). These relationships are born out of a productive prayer life.

Our prayers must not be based on misconceptions and false perceptions. We should never try to manipulate the lives of others or insist on changing them according to our own desires.

Our strongholds of rigidity, denial, emotional isolation, and silence must be recognized, broken down, and confessed in repentance to Father God. **Rigidity** renders a person inflexible, suppressing the ministry of our constant transformation. **Denial** opens the door for self-deception, repudiating the truth which sets us free. **Emotional isolation** causes us to be subject to hardness of heart, overruling our compassion for others. **Silence** stops the communication of our faith preventing our true fellowship with God and man.

The Holy Spirit brings revelation, Jesus breaks down every wall, and our Heavenly Father restores and brings salvation to our every destruction. He always wants you and me to be aware that we represent Him right where we live, and wherever He sends us. These strongholds inhibit good communication skills, and hinder our testimony of a life of peace and victory.

There is a life in the prayer closet and beyond. In Matthew 6 Jesus teaches on the subject of prayer. He warns us of behaving as hypocrites who love to make a show of their religiosity. Jesus teaches us to go into the prayer closet — He promised that our Father Who sees in secret will reward us openly. "Going into the prayer closet" is easily understood. Most conscientious believers are willing to follow these instructions about praying privately. How does God reward us openly? I believe that most of us who have prayed diligently for our families would say that our reward is noticeable behavioral "changes."

God desires to bring about changes in our homes, as well as to develop within us the desire to live as fully mature followers of our Lord Jesus Christ. That which is openly manifested in us should be the fruit of the Spirit, those godly characteristics which influence others and draw them to Jesus Christ.

What does my behavior reflect to those with whom I come in contact? Do I wear my prayer life as a badge of self-righteousness where I am the only one who knows what godly behavior is?

God has said that the spouse may be saved by the godly behavior of the believer. What does our behavior say about us? Do we wear our prayer life as a badge, proclaiming either overtly or sub-consciously to all about our sacrificial life in the prayer closet; or do we demonstrate righteousness, peace and joy in the Holy Ghost to our loved ones? These are questions that each of us must look at honestly.

It is our responsibility to be sensitive to the voice of God and responsive to His call to intercession both in the prayer closet and beyond. God wants to use us as channels of answered prayer. In our daily lives we exemplify the changes which took place through our diligent prayer time with the Father God.

Remember, the seeds of prayer that you have sown on behalf of others will profit you — will change your false beliefs — will destroy your past defenses and enable you to complete your ministry of reconciliation.

12
PRAYER TIME:
Joy or Bondage?

Today we are hearing testimonies from many who are rising early in the morning to pray. The testimonies are very inspiring as we are told of the benefits of rising early to seek the Lord. Manifold scriptures are given to support this practice and it seems that everyone who hears gets excited and makes the decision to adapt his or her lifestyle to include early morning prayer time.

How early one gets up to pray has become a topic of conversation in some Christian circles. The emphasis has changed from praying to how *early* that praying should be done. Many people are quietly going about obeying God, praying early each day as the Spirit has directed. Some are rising early, even going to their churches, and have experienced great changes in their lives. Among these, however, there are those who have unconsciously become prideful, boasting about their achievement; while others are suffering from self-condemnation, wondering why they have not been able to conquer their sleeping habits.

. . . as many as are led by the Spirit of God, they are the sons of God (Rom. 8:14 KJV). If you believe that God desires you to rise early to keep your appointment with Him, you must obey. However, if you are struggling to meet someone else's expectations, be set free today to follow the Spirit of the Lord.

I believe that you must be led by the Spirit of God concerning both the time and the duration of your prayer sessions.

How long should we pray? Jesus said to His disciples in the Garden of Gethsemane, . . . **Are you so utterly unable to stay awake and watch with Me for one hour?** (Matt. 26:40). This statement has become the *rhema* of God to many people and they are praying at least one hour each day. If this verse has not become revelation knowledge to you personally, or if you are just trying to imitate what others are doing, then your prayer time can easily become a drudgery and just another work of the flesh. Prayer is habit-forming. Those who make the decision to pray one hour soon find that time increased. The more you pray, the more you desire to pray.

Christians must be led by the Spirit of God in the matter of prayer. I urge you to depend on the Holy Spirit Who knows you and your individual personality, lifestyle and schedule. It is He Who will instruct you and show you the pathway of prayer.

What time do I pray? Is early morning the only time to pray? If I don't get up early to pray, is it a sign that I don't love God as much as I should? Is Satan interfering with my prayer life, stealing my time by making it difficult for me to get out of bed? Will God hear me at 10:00 a.m., at 1:00 p.m., or at 9:00 p.m. as quickly and clearly as He will at 5:00 a.m.?

Satan is taking advantage of many believers with his subtlety by exercising spirits of condemnation. Praying out of a sense of guilt or according to another's standards can make prayer a bondage rather than a privilege. For instance, if a person sleeps past his self-appointed hour of prayer, he can easily become consumed with his failure to get out of bed when he's supposed to. A pattern of negative thinking can be immediately set in motion to play havoc with his prayer time. Also if, for some reason, his allotted prayer time is cut short, he feels guilty and his confidence in God can be shaken for that day.

Does God command everyone to rise before daybreak to pray, regardless of individual and family lifestyles or job situations? I don't think so.

We do need to find time alone with the Father daily, whether it is early in the morning, in the middle of the afternoon, or late in the evening. It is easier for me if I begin my day with prayer. The first thing I do upon waking is greet the Father, Jesus and the Holy Spirit. The time is not as important as the circumstances and the state of our own heart and mind. The following are examples of two people who spend time with the Father, fellowshipping with Him and praying for others — yet they are totally different in their time and approach.

Several years ago my mom, Donnis Griffin, asked the Holy Spirit to reveal to her a time she could be alone with God. That was not as simple as it may sound because my dad had retired from pastoral work and was always home. But since Mom always says, ''Don't ask God a question unless you want to know the answer," she was open to whatever the Lord might present. The Holy Spirit responded by telling her to get up and pray each morning while Dad was out jogging. That was fine, except that he was an early riser — one of those types who believes that when you get up you should be instantly awake all over — spirit, soul and body.

Mom was a late sleeper. However, she had asked the Lord for an answer and got it, so she was determined that she would obey God. For a few days she had to be awakened, but soon she found herself waking up even before Dad because the Lord had created a desire in her to get up and spend time in His presence. Her time alone with God was and is the most important time of her day. Early morning prayer has now become a way of life for her. The answers to her prayers have been remarkable and have caused much thanksgiving to God the Father. As a result, her fellowship with God has grown more and more intimate.

My mother shared this experience with me in the very beginning of her newly appointed time with God the Father. I became very excited about it and decided that if she could do that, then so could I. My self-appointed time with God early every morning did not last too long. When I got to comparing lifestyles, I found that Mom was going to bed very early in the evening in order to get up before daylight. However, this early rising had become such a part of her daily routine that even when she was up late at night for some reason, it didn't stop her from rising early the next morning to spend her time with God. As I looked at my schedule I discovered that my lifestyle was quite different from my mother's. My family and church situations required that I be up late at night more often than not.

Condemnation flooded me again and again as I tried to make myself get up to conform to my mother's routine. "Others get up early for their prayer time, why can't I?" I asked myself. "What's wrong with me? Why can't I conquer this thing which causes me to sleep past the time everyone else is already praying?"

I felt as though I had failed God when I had not risen early (at 4:30 or 5:00 a.m.) to pray. If I didn't get up at that time, then I could not get in the number of hours that the others were spending in prayer. For example, my mother prays until she is through — however long that may take. Others were letting me know that they were praying for four to six hours each day and that I was not being obedient to God if I didn't do the same. I felt a burden of guilt and self-condemnation. (This burden was not put on me by my mom who always said that her schedule was given to her by the Holy Spirit and that each person must ask Him what He desires them to do. Not everyone allows you this freedom to hear from God for yourself.)

In the end, the Father and I worked it out. I set my clock for a certain hour that is compatible with my lifestyle. However, many mornings the Holy Spirit calls my name before the clock-radio sounds off. Remember that God is all the while effectually at work in you — energizing and creating in you the power and desire — both to will and to work for His good pleasure and satisfaction and delight. (Phil. 2:13.) He will do His part; it is your responsibility to cooperate. **If you are willing and obedient, you shall eat the good of the land** (Is. 1:19).

The second example is a gentleman here in Atlanta who has been used mightily by God to influence the lives of many people who have frequented his place of business. He has many testimonies to share as a result of prayer and being obedient to the Spirit. He has seen many lives changed, people who have received salvation and healing. His time to pray is 9:00 p.m. If you ask this man to pray for you, you can know that at some point between nine and ten o'clock in the evening he is praying.

Jesus prayed all night and in the early morning, before ministering and after ministering. The Father's ears are open to the prayers of His people regardless of when we pray. Jesus said that we are to pray at all times, and Paul reinforced this teaching when he later wrote that we should pray **without ceasing** (1 Thess. 5:17 KJV).

I once heard an expression which has become a part of my vocabulary: ''Continually practice the presence of Jesus.'' The important thing is that you and I are to give the Lord preeminence in our lives. The Father is not limited to only certain hours of the day; He is always attentive to the prayers of His people. He never slumbers or sleeps.

Donnis Griffin, whom I have cited as an example of an early morning pray-er, was free to fit this type and time of prayer into her lifestyle. My mother's decision fit into a pattern that put no pressure on the lifestyle which she and my dad had chosen for themselves. In fact, now they are both ''early to bed and early to rise'' people, working even more closely in the beautiful harmony and agreement which they have experienced for most of their fifty-four years together.

It was my husband, Everette, who spoke the words that set me free: "Pressure is not from God. He will not require something of you that applies pressure to you and which then in turn applies pressure to your family causing everyone to be miserable."

The peace of God which we had enjoyed for many years had been interrupted by my attempt at early-morning prayer. That peace was restored when I chose to follow after the Spirit and not after man. Prayer time should be a time of joy where you gain strength even while praying for others. When you are led by the Spirit in your prayer time, pressures are relieved rather than intensified.

You will have to make a decision to spend time in prayer. Effective praying does require a made-up mind, but it is not attained through sheer will power. It is an activity which must be motivated by the love of God, for God, and for others. It is in your prayer time where human weaknesses are often exposed, but always remember that Jesus said, . . . **My grace is sufficient for thee: for my strength is made perfect in weakness** . . . (2 Cor. 12:9). You can obey the call to prayer.

Satan would discourage you and steal your time with God, if possible. Ask the Holy Spirit for direction, obey Him and God's grace will enable you to follow through at your divinely appointed prayer time. You are not sufficient of yourself to think anything as of yourself; but your sufficiency is of God. (2 Cor. 3:5.) It is God's ability in you which will motivate you to a life of prayer. It is His Word which will light your pathway and the Holy Spirit Who will take the words of Jesus and reveal them to you. The disciples asked Jesus to teach them to pray. His teaching in word and practice is our example for prayer today. Do not neglect your time alone with God in Bible study and prayer for this is the key to released power and praying prayers that avail much.

Many people in our Bible studies have listened to various teachers and struggled to pray earlier each morning and to intercede or to pray in the spirit a set number of hours — following the routines of others. It has caused much thanksgiving to God as we have seen these people set free — going from bondage to joy in their prayer time. Whom the Son has set free is free indeed! (John 8:36.) Rejoice in your time with the Father God — whenever that time may be.

CONCLUSION: CONDITIONS FOR ANSWERED PRAYER

Everyone who prays desires that his prayers be answered. Some fail to pray because they do not know their spiritual authority and the power of prayer. The laws governing prayer are found in the Scriptures. Obeying them results in answered prayers. These laws are not bondage, but freedom to give and to receive.

The Bible is a revelation of who we are; it establishes our rights and privileges in Christ Jesus. Your particular need is covered in this great Book of the ages. Study the Bible until you are fully persuaded that God will answer your petitions:

> **And this is the confidence that we have in him, that, if we ask any thing according to his will, he heareth us:**
>
> **And if we know that he hear us, whatsoever we ask, we know that we have the petitions that we desired of him.**
>
> **1 John 5:14,15 KJV**

Check out your motives regarding your present "need." Is your prayer request made for the good of

141

others or only for self-gratification? Jesus admonished His followers to give. In Luke 6 it is perfectly clear that we will receive according to the measure given, whether it be mercy, judgment, condemnation, forgiveness or material goods. Rid yourself of all selfishness, doing unto others as you would have them do unto you. (Luke 6:31.) God will answer your prayers if you believe on the name of His Son and love your neighbor as yourself. (1 John 3:17-24.)

Renew your mind, resisting the temptation to be squeezed into the conceptual mold of this present evil world. After ridding yourself of wrong motives and attitudes, establish that it is God's will to meet your need. Take authority over your thought life. Do not entertain fear nor engage in rigidity, denial, or emotional isolation. The promised land of rest and peace belonged to the children of Israel, but they failed "to enter therein because of their unbelief." (Heb. 3:19 KJV.)

Pray According to God's Word

Submit to God and His will, which is recorded in His Word, and all doubts and fears will flee. (James 4:7; 1 Pet. 5:8,9.) James said that a double-minded man receives nothing from God. When you ask in faith, without wavering, you will receive "the great recompence of reward" — your prayer will be answered. (Heb. 10:19-36 KJV.)

After you have prayed according to the will and purpose of God, you must cast down every imagination, theory, religious precept, philosophy and reasoning which sets itself against the knowledge of God —

His Word. (2 Cor. 10:5.) Most people have formed patterns of thinking which are contrary to the ways of God. It is your responsibility to bring every thought into captivity, destroying every psychological stronghold with the Gospel of Christ, establishing a new fortress for Kingdom living. This means casting aside worry and anxiety about the outcome of that for which you have prayed. (1 Pet. 5:7; Phil. 4:6.) Refuse to see past mistakes as failures; consider them as stepping-stones promulgating you from glory to glory by the Holy Spirit. Circumstances are created through the decision-making process. Decisions should always be guided by the Holy Spirit, however the results of our choices sometimes conflict with spiritual laws already in motion. Should you find yourself in a desperate situation, look to God for your deliverance. Believe that God has already delivered you from all your destructions. (Ps. 107:20 AMP.) Through the eye of faith, look at things that are not seen rather than things that are temporal.

Abraham, the father of faith, praised God for the blessing even before it was physically manifested. (Rom. 4:20.) Praise God for the answer, exercise patience; wait for the answer to your prayer in peace and confidence. (Heb. 10:35,37.)

Forgiveness — A Key to Answered Prayer

Jesus said, **"Listen to me! You can pray for anything, and if you believe, you have it; it's yours! But when you are praying, first forgive anyone you are holding a grudge against . . . ."** (Mark 11:24,25 TLB) Understanding the process of true forgiveness paves the way for answered prayer. When someone has wronged you, be honest with yourself; express your true feelings and deal truly. Allow the anointing that is upon Jesus to bind up and heal your brokenness. Receive your healing which will enable you to pull down the wall of emotional isolation permitting others back into your heart. Forgiveness does not always dissipate a memory, but it does eradicate the sting. An intercessor's prayer life is dependent on having a pure heart before God and a clear conscience. A sincere desire to have a successful prayer life necessitates looking beyond situations, problems and circumstances. Forgive and praise. Call "the things which be not as though they were." (Rom. 4:16-22.) Add to your faithful praise patience, awaiting the answer to your prayer in peace and confidence. (Heb. 10:35,37.)

Abide in Christ

Jesus reveals the all-inclusive condition of answered prayer in His message to His disciples on the way to the Garden of Gethsemane: **If ye abide in me, and my words abide in you, ye shall ask what ye will, and it shall be done unto you** (John 15:7 KJV). This is an amazing promise which Jesus so boldly makes to us. He not only gives us this promise, but also prays for us, **That they all may be one; as thou, Father, art in me, and I in thee, that they also may be one in us . . .** (John 17:21 KJV).

*This is the key to answered prayer: abiding in Him —
the true Vine.*

Jesus stated that He is the Vine and we are the branches. (John 15:5.) The branch cannot bear fruit of itself, but must receive its life from the vine. Our Lord promised that if we would abide in Him, we would produce fruit — prayer fruit. The fruit of the Spirit is listed in Galatians 5:22,23; here Jesus is speaking of prayer fruit. It is an absolute prerequisite that we abide in the Vine and bear fruit, knowing that without Him we can do nothing.

Many have overlooked one statement that Jesus made in this chapter. He said that if we do not bear fruit we will be cut off. (John 15:6.) Prayer is essential to the eternal welfare of each individual believer. Man has been created for God's pleasure and to bring glory to Him: **Herein is my Father glorified, that ye bear much fruit; so shall ye be my disciples** (John 15:8 KJV).

Jesus said that He came to finish the works of the Father. (John 4:34.) We must work while it is yet day for the night is coming when no man can work. (John 9:4.) We must follow the example of Jesus and finish the work which remains — bearing prayer-fruit, preparing the way of the Lord. Be available not only to pray, but also to serve the Father in any area of ministry. A fruit-bearing intercessor is a joyful intercessor.

After Jesus reveals the conditions of answered prayer, He declares the blessings of abiding in Him. One of those blessings is joy unspeakable and full of glory. (John 15:11.)

Obey His Commandments

The first prerequisite is that we dwell in God's love by obeying His commandments. (John 15:12-15.) Just as Jesus kept the Father's commandments, so must we. He assures us that if we abide in the Vine, producing

145

prayer-fruit and obeying the Father, His joy will remain in us and our joy will be full.

It is impossible to be truly joyful without truly loving. That's why the Lord's second injunction is that we love one another as He has loved us. (John 15:12). The greatest expression of love is the laying down of one's life for his friends.

Sowing and Reaping

The law of sowing and reaping works in the prayer arena. There is a time to sow and a time to reap. **[Remember] this: he who sows sparingly and grudgingly will also reap sparingly and grudgingly, and he who sows generously and that blessings may come to someone, will also reap generously and with blessings** (2 Cor. 9:6).

Don't wait for problems to force you to pray. Be ready for prayer assignments from the Holy Spirit. **Don't be weary in prayer; keep at it; watch for God's answers and remember to be thankful when they come.** (Col. 4:2 TLB). It is in the good times that seed is sown; then when the harvest comes, you will be ready to reap it. When you sow in prayer, God will put you into someone's prayers and you will reap the benefits of someone else's intercession. Without sowing, there will be no reaping.

The liberal person shall be enriched, and he who waters shall himself be watered (Prov. 11:25.) Water is a symbol of the Holy Spirit, and as you pray water will flow out into the desert into the lives of others.

146

Recently my mother, Donnis Griffin, experienced a great trial when she was attacked with a physical illness. Early morning always finds her worshiping her heavenly Father and interceding for others, as rivers of living water flow from within her innermost being. As a result, any time she needs to drink from the living water, it is there for her.

The week this problem began, a pastor's wife called me to ask about my mother. She related how an image of Donnis kept coming before her in prayer. God had raised up someone to stand in the gap who did not even know what was happening.

The pain was almost more than Donnis could bear, but through the intercession of another she could maintain "the good fight of faith." (1 Tim. 6:12.) During the first week of this trial, she concealed her pain from those in her household, going right on about her normal activities — cooking meals, taking a neighbor to the hospital, shopping with her week-long visitor and keeping up the solid front of joy. God began to raise up other intercessors to pray for her. Over the next few weeks, family and friends entered with her into "the good fight of faith." She never waivered in her faith, and God sent forth His Word and healed her. (Ps. 107:20.)

Sow in season and you will reap the harvest.

Seek First the Kingdom of God

Seek first the Kingdom of God, and His righteousness. (Matt. 6:33.) God's Kingdom is not ushered in with visible signs. (Luke 17:20.) It is a mystery. Natural man (the unsaved person) does not receive the things of the Spirit of God, for they are foolishness to him. (1 Cor. 2:14.) However, I have good news; it has been given to the Christian to know the mystery of the Kingdom. (Mark 4:11.) This knowledge is spiritually discerned.

If you are not praying for your family or your church, begin now. Pray for those who persecute you. Pray for all churches, all denominations, all nations. The more you pray, the more the Holy Spirit will expand your capacity for prayer. Become sensitive to Kingdom situations, receiving and cultivating the true intercession of Jesus.

REFERENCES

REFERENCES

Scripture quotations marked KJV are taken from the King James Version of the Bible.

Scripture quotations marked NAS are taken from the New American Standard Bible, Copyright © The Lockman Foundation, 1960, 1962, 1963, 1968, 1971, 1972, 1973, 1975, 1977.

Scripture quotations marked TLB are taken from the Living Bible © 1971. Used by permission of Tyndale House Publishers, Inc., Wheaton, IL 60189. All rights reserved.

Scripture quotations marked NIV are taken from the Holy Bible, New International Version. Copyright © 1973, 1978, 1984 by International Bible Society. Used by permission of Zondervan Bible Publishers.

Scriptures marked Phil are taken from The New Testament in Modern English, by J. B. Phillips, Ed. The Macmillan Publishing Company, Inc. Copyright © 1958, 1960, 1972 by J. B. Phillips. Reprinted with permission.

Germaine Griffin Copeland is Founder and President of Word Ministries, Inc. As the daughter of a Church of God minister, she knew in her early teens that God was calling her into the ministry. Only after she was married and had four children did Germaine realize her desperate need to know God personally. As she reached out to Him, He moved in and "old things passed away, and behold all things became new."

In 1969 Germaine began to grow in the knowledge of God's love and in the reality of overcoming faith. In 1972 God opened doors for her to share what she had learned. She began teaching with Women's Aglow Fellowship and within a few years became a renowned conference speaker. Later, Word Ministries, Inc. was formed and in 1980 published *Prayers That Avail Much*. Since that time, Germaine has shared her love of God with truth and in simplicity to many in congregations and in many seminars throughout the country. In 1984 she was called to the office of pastor of Word of Life Christian Fellowship in Smyrna, Georgia.

Today Germaine balances her home and ministry with great wisdom and love. She ministers God's Word and the gifts of His Holy Spirit with tenderness and a deep desire to meet the needs of His people.

**You may contact
Word Ministries
by writing:**

Word Ministries, Inc.
38 Sloan Street
Roswell, GA 30075

*Please include
your prayer requests
and comments when you write.*

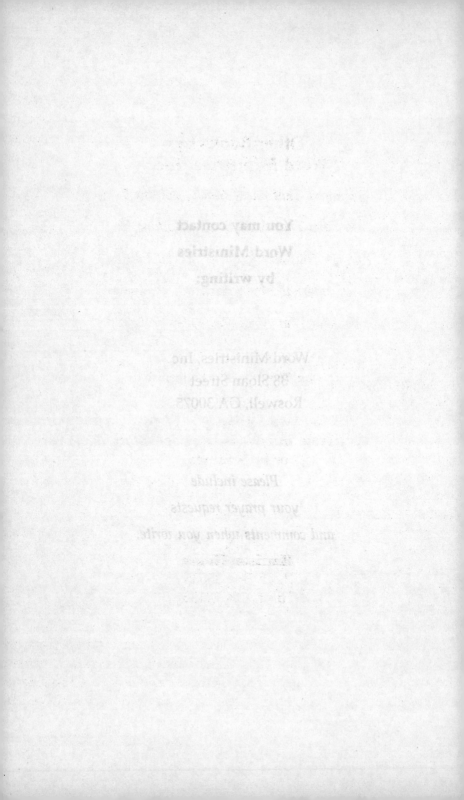

Other Books by
Word Ministries, Inc.

Prayers That Avail Much, Volume I

Prayers That Avail Much, Volume II

Prayers That Avail Much, Special Edition

Prayers That Avail Much, for Mothers

Prayers That Avail Much, for Fathers

Oraciones Con Poder
(Prayers That Avail Much, Spanish)

Available from your local bookstore
or by writing:

Harrison House
P. O. Box 35035
Tulsa, OK 74135

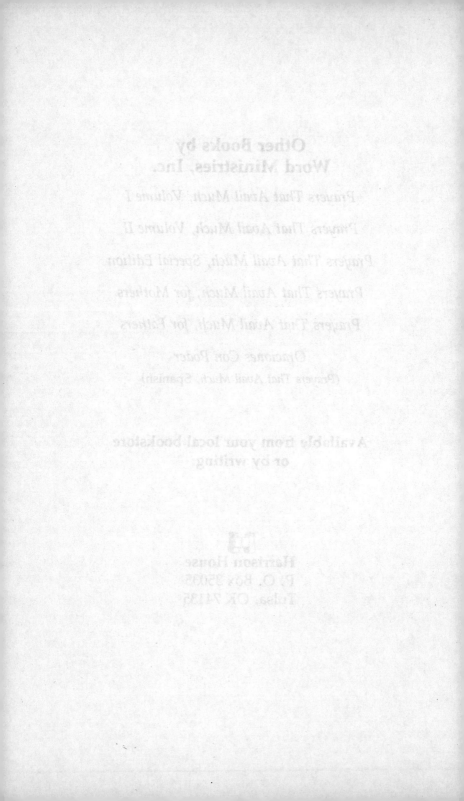

For additional copies
of this book
in Canada contact:

Word Alive
P. O. Box 670
Niverville, Manitoba
CANADA R0A 1EO

The Harrison House Vision

Proclaiming the truth and the power
Of the Gospel of Jesus Christ
With excellence;

Challenging Christians to
Live victoriously,
Grow spiritually,
Know God Intimately.